Crohn's

Life in remission

This book is dedicated to my beloved friend M who sadly passed away just before I managed to get this book ready to be published. I would like to dedicate this book to M and her family as a way of remembering some of her memories with me, she became a very close friend due to my illness and I would also like to take this time to say thank you to M and her family for helping me to become the person I am today and for giving me permission to continue with this book

XXXXXXXXXXXXXXXXXXX

Contents

Prologue

Writing my first book has made me realise that I have managed to find a way of releasing my feelings positively without having to worry others around me, but being able to share my experiences so that I can hopefully find a way to help others to understand my illnesses and to also reassure others that they are not alone.

As I enjoyed writing my first book, I decided to write a sequel so that you can continue to follow my journey through to the next stages of my life from where book one ended until April 2015, and to see how I coped; if you too are a fellow sufferer then hopefully it will offer some comfort.

I had so much positive encouragement and feedback from my first book and it gave me the strength to write this follow up book. So here it is. I have had the ideas for this book whilst writing my first, so I hope you all find it an "easy to follow" read and that it gives you an insight of how Crohn's affects us daily and throughout our life. This is not a short term illness that goes away and never returns. It can appear whenever it wants to and normally when sufferers least expect it.

I hope you all enjoy the book and continue to understand a little of what Crohn's sufferers can experience.

Note to reader

I wanted to say that these are based on my experiences and that everyone may experience things differently, please do not treat my book as a way of getting answers for any symptoms you may get, please ensure you seek appropriate medical advice still. However at the same time I hope it gives some relief that you or a friend or relative are not alone with how they feel.

I have written this as a 'diary' style, it wasn't intentional but I hope that you still enjoy it as some things were written in present tense as I wrote parts of this as I was experiencing different situations.

As I begin to write this story, I was in remission and I still am but who knows where I will be at the end of it.

Brief History

In case anyone has not read my first story, here is a short recap of what my life and health was like before this point.

- 2002 – Married John
- 2007- Our daughter was born – she was not an easy labour and I haemorrhaged badly, needing a blood transfusion
- 2010 – Our son was born – he was born by planned caesarean two weeks early as I had placenta praevia and bled continuously throughout this pregnancy, required a blood transfusion
- May 2011 – Started experiencing symptoms such as fatigue, diarrhoea and nausea, losing weight
- Christmas 2011 – Symptoms continued but started to get blood in stools
- March 2012 - Finally referred to hospital after endless doctors visits.
- May 2012 – Flexi sigmoidoscopy procedure
- June 2012 – Diagnosed with Crohn's and had CT scan and blood tests to start on treatments,
- August 2012 – Treatment was making me ill so had to stop and also referred to hospital management team regarding additional concerning symptoms
- September 2012 - Referred to a colorectal surgeon and seen by him
- October 2012 – Colonoscopy procedure and MRI scan, also admitted to hospital
- November 2012 – had planned bowel resection, fistula and my right ovary was removed
- December 2012 - During recovery in hospital my bowel perforated so an emergency bowel resection took place and a temporary ileostomy was formed
- April 2013 – Ileostomy reversal operation took place
- May 2013 – Anaemic so had 4 iron infusions at hospital
- June 2013 – Ultra sound showed a cyst like shape
- June 2013 - MRI scan
- July 2013 - Clinic apt showed it was a fluid build up from operations, was in remission with Crohn's.

- July 2013 - Saw dietician and counsellors for various reasons
- September 2013 - Referred to Rheumatology due to joint pain
- October 2013 – Seen by Rheumatology and diagnosed with Enteropathic Arthritis brought on by Crohn's. Started on Methotrexate, however due to nausea and reactions I switched from tablet form to injection form.

I hope this helps you all to understand this second part of my story. So much has happened in such a short space of time that it is not until it is written down like this I realise what has happened. Living with it and reading it are two different things; I do not want people to feel sorry for me but to be inspired that the second part of my journey is about how I have found a way of moving forward even with all that has gone on. It is possible for anyone to overcome such obstacles, however like I said in the first book everyone's experiences are so different and the journey and recovery times may differ greatly. As long as people offer support and do not judge anyone for the length of time it takes us or for the way we live with our illness, then we are able to achieve anything in life, but mostly we need to learn to accept ourselves and then others will accept us too.

My story

One

In March 2014, the waiting game is beginning again, but this time round it feels different. I suppose looking back at all that I have been through, this time round should be a piece of cake. There are times when I get scared, but the more positive thoughts are pushing the scary ones away. I am determined this time to look at my life and my difficulties in a more positive light. Each day the light at the end of the tunnel is drawing closer; however I am sure there are many more obstacles to overcome yet.

I am trying to enjoy the Easter holidays as much as I can; my little girl caught chicken pox on her first day of the holidays and missed her dance shows, but once she was okay we went out and had a shopping day out and lunch in a Chinese. I made sure I was careful what I ate but I still felt yucky and bloated afterwards. However it was worth it to see her happy face gleaming for once over the past two weeks. I have never seen her in so much pain before and she was crying all the time from the pain but most of all being upset that she was unable to perform on stage with her friends.

It was an emotional time but she received so many kind messages and presents from some of her friends and it brought back memories of when I was ill in hospital and when my friends and family did the same for me. It is times like these that make me appreciate what we have and how many lovely friends we have made since moving from Essex to Norfolk. Of course we miss our other friends but we definitely made the right step as my daughter also has another family, her dance friends.

Over the Easter Holidays we saw our family and our little boy had a birthday party to go to. Although the majority of it we were housebound due to the dreaded chicken pox as our son also caught it. He was very unwell with it as he had a reaction to the chicken pox, which also triggered two serious asthma attacks; still we found a lot of things to do at home, such as painting, Hama beads, drawing, DVD days, garden time, and puzzles. It was nice to do the simple cheap activities and I realised that to have fun does not mean that we have to spend money, and when on a tight budget this was the ideal fun time.

The cabin fever towards the end of all this was unbearable and I needed a lot of help getting my eldest back to school as because my son was still so ill it was impossible to get him out for me to do so. There was a lot of organising amongst my parents and friends but we managed. I felt so grateful knowing I have some very reliable and caring friends around. It was around this time that I noticed that my joints had improved. Which I was pleased about as I was worried how I would cope with being a nurse to my children. However the pain in my stomach remained as bad as ever; even when sticking to my diets and doing my best to drink as much water as possible. However the constant caring for two ill children over a long period of time with my constant fatigue exhausted me even further.

I seem to be constantly tired and fatigued and can doze off unexpectedly which is a worry at times especially when I am alone with the children. As I have said though this time round I feel stressed and anxious but it is nowhere near as bad as I felt two years ago. Although the past two years were rough, it has certainly given me a good platform for the next round of hurdles and I feel more certain that I can overcome these as well.

Two

In May 2014 the hospital appointments have begun again. My first appointment was my routine blood test, and after two attempts they managed to find a vein and get some. Apparently it is quite common with Crohn's to have poor veins. I even made sure that I drank plenty of water but it still did not help. Although by now I am used to these tests so it did not bother me. My only issues are after the tests I can sometime bruise easily from the needles. This is just a side effect of long term steroid use and something you get used to.

My next appointment was at the hospital with the Rheumatology specialist nurses. I did not have to wait long and I was surprisingly seen in record time too. At the time of my appointment my joints were good due to the change of weather as it was becoming warmer. I was advised to get some heat gel packs for the cold seasons which can be placed in gloves. She examined all my joints and I had to score myself on how much my joints affected me daily and once the points were calculated she told me some surprising news that my Arthritis was in remission; I was so pleased as I knew it would mean no increase in dose as I struggled with the nausea last time. My blood results were perfect so all was good; my next appointment is with the Rheumatology consultant in June and I next see the Rheumatology nurses in August. I was very pleased as it did not just mean that my treatment of Methotrexate remained the same but also my appointments were becoming less frequent.

I am now waiting for my next appointment which I am getting quite nervous about; it is with my Gastroenterologist. I saw him last in November 2013 and I was advised to try diets to improve and decrease my stomach pain before needing the toilet. However the diets have not helped that dramatically. Nothing has alleviated many of my symptoms. I remember him telling me that if it does not help they would have to consider another operation to look at what is going on and to repair the adhesions if that is what is causing the pain. I have no idea how this appointment will go, but I have a long list of other symptoms too and a list of questions so I just hope I manage to get to discuss it all.

It gets very frustrating as I would love to be completely symptom free; I now have the Arthritis under control but I am now back to sorting my stomach out. I hope that it will not alternate and that I manage to resolve both illnesses soon as I would feel I have achieved something and it would be more noticeable. However to look at me, I suppose for others no one sees the changes as I still look the same, but how I feel has changed. It is nice not having the burning pain when I walk or when I plait our daughter's hair or when I type or open cans or carry saucepans. Don't get me wrong, I have some days when I notice some pains and my joints become swollen, but it is reassuring to know that it does not last too long anymore and with a lot of rest I can get my joints back to feeling ok pretty quickly.

Luckily before my appointment we have a bank holiday weekend to enjoy; we have a couple of things planned and my husband John is off for 5 days so we can have some quality time together as a family. Even though I am in pain, this time round I am dealing with it differently by distracting myself and trying to ignore the constant pains. It seems to help but I do not also want to distract myself too much and forget about it as I know left untreated could make it worse for the future, so I have started to write all my questions and symptoms down for it, something I would suggest others to do too.

Even though I was suffering with pain and bloating, we still managed to enjoy the weekend; we went to the cinema as a family and had lunch out. We also spent a lot of time in the garden and went and spent the day in Lincolnshire with John's family. It was a great weekend and I ensured that my Crohn's and symptoms were not going to spoil it! It's surprising what you can achieve when you put your mind to it. It would be hard to do this 24/7 but for special occasions it is very much worth it.

My Gastroenterology appointment was here; we discussed my current symptoms and they advised me that I should have a colonoscopy to rule out any active

Crohn's; if there is no Crohn's active then there are a few more medications to try and stop my cramping, pain and bloating. I visited Gastroenterology to hand in my colonoscopy request form. Two weeks later I heard from them and we arranged the date of my colonoscopy. I now have to wait until June 16th to go for this. Even though I have had two before, these never get easier as you know what to expect. I am dreading the preparation as I get bad stomach cramps without taking laxatives (these are used in preparation for a colonoscopy to clear out your bowels). However it needs to be done so that I can find out what it is that is causing my symptoms. The things we all have to do just to find out what's wrong.

On the 19th May it was world IBD (Inflammatory Bowel Disease) day; I wore my purple nail varnish and my daughter wore purple hair bands to school to raise awareness. I also did my awareness cards on Facebook which is something that the charity had organised to raise awareness through social media. It was a time for anyone who suffers with Inflammatory Bowel Disease to write their story on a card of their diagnosis, any surgeries and treatments they are on and can be shared on the Charity page publicly. I had a couple of lovely messages from friends and two people even asked me about how I have coped in the past two years. It was good to see my friends not feeling embarrassed or ashamed in asking me, I made the first move making my Crohn's public so it was good that they asked me too in person as I did not feel so alone or so "alien" to people.

I have been concentrating on my gardens at home and it is nice to finally have the energy and joints to manage it. It is a great way to release my feelings and a place to think things through and to be myself without hiding away and pretending all is ok. I love gardening and it has helped me to relax more. I am slowly getting there and I am now trying to find inspiration and ideas on what plants to grow in my garden. I aim to buy a few each season so that I have always got flowers in my garden. My children have helped too and it is nice to see us all work together to achieve something pretty for us all to enjoy. Things are finally getting easier at home as the children are getting older and able to help me more and are becoming more confident and independent. I still struggle at times but I feel this is the medication affecting my hormones more and I try to explain this as best as I can to the children without worrying them.

I went back to the doctors due to the constant fatigue as it was getting significantly worse. The dozing unexpectedly was happening more and more. She said that she wanted to wait until after my colonoscopy to make any necessary referrals or changes to medication as she felt it could be either Crohn's fatigue, or if the colonoscopy shows that the Crohn's is inactive then it could be Chronic Fatigue Syndrome (CFS, otherwise known as ME). I came away shocked as she said it would mean a referral to the CFS clinic. She also wants to see what it shows before she reviews my birth control pills and whether I should change to a different one, due to my hormones being unbalanced and still getting a lot of Crohn's problems and pains around the time I should be having a break.

I felt deflated as I now was unsure how I felt about my colonoscopy and whether I wanted it to show Crohn's or not as it could mean another referral and another doctor and as a result, more appointments again. However I also felt relieved knowing that I am not imagining my symptoms.

All this time I was pushing myself away from people and I didn't speak about my illness as often, not because I was embarrassed (as I always see it as raising awareness), but more due to the fact that I did not want to burden anyone with my problems, there are people out there suffering so much worse than me. My special friend M is always there and we still talk near enough every day; we always manage to cheer each other up and I managed to visit her too for lunch. It was a lovely afternoon and we always manage to continue our chats from wherever we left off before. Like I said in my first book, M was like a blessing in disguise when I saw her in hospital after my emergency operation, I still feel as if she was put opposite me in that hospital bay for a reason. She has helped me become a more positive person and has taught me so much about life in such a short space of time.

My next appointment was finally here, and that is with the dietician. By this point my love - hate relationship with food was getting worse, and I realised that my symptoms had not changed much from when I first saw her. I was still going from diarrhoea to constipation, still having urgencies to need the toilet fast as well as the nausea, bloating and stomach pains and cramps. My bowel movements were anywhere between two to three times a day to two to three times a week. We spoke a lot about ways of altering the fodmap diet I was currently trying but in the end we discussed the possibility of a liquid diet and then under close supervision an elimination diet which is where you slowly reintroduce foods and see what exactly I react to. Some would feel quite shocked but I actually agreed to do this, I have heard a lot about these diets on my Facebook Cohn's support groups so kind of already knew what to expect, however she explained what would happen and that I would need to do the liquid diet for at least two weeks to gain any benefit from it. By this point I was happy to starve for the rest of my life as long as the hunger was taken away as I am so confused with what foods are causing what reactions and why I just seem to bloat badly regardless of what I eat and drink. She said she would want to wait until after my colonoscopy and in the mean-time will speak to my Gastroenterologist to discuss this further with him. Once I have had my colonoscopy I will see him as well as the dietician again to discuss further options with them.

Between this appointment and June 16th was like torture; I ended up getting severe pains but it did not stop me from doing some practice walks as the four of us are going to London for an organised CCUK (Crohn's and Colitis UK) charity event, where we are walking 5k around London. We have raised £200 so far for the charity and due to my severe fatigue I felt it was best to try and walk 5k a few times before hand. My friend does a lot of running so she found a good route and we walked it together. It was a lovely morning and I thoroughly enjoyed it. We plan on doing a couple more to keep practising. However I came home and ended up having an unexpected period. I felt deflated as the pill was finally working but it did explain my hormones as well as the severe pain. I ended up needing to call the doctors as I was unsure what to do due to taking the pill constantly. However I was advised to take a break from the pill for 5 days and then continue on day 5 or 6 of the break. My Crohn's is flaring badly whilst on this break and it proves why I so desperately need to be on a pill constantly. I know I am not alone with this issue as this is discussed regularly by most women on the support groups. I feel reassured that I am not suffering with this alone.

I now have 5 days until my colonoscopy; I read up on my procedure notes and I start starving for it on Saturday. I feel scared as my parents are on holiday whilst I have it and I am slightly anxious due to my husband having to pick up our kiddies in between it all so I hope that because my husband is not going to be there for the whole appointment that they will still sedate me. However what will be will be on the day, I may need to ask favours from friends but we shall have to wait and see.

Three

So the preparation for my colonoscopy has begun. Fortunately I have been flaring due to an unexpected period, so this has made me lose my appetite which helped me with the starvation part of the preparation. On June 15th (Father's Day), I had to start taking Picolax (laxatives to clear my bowel out ready for the procedure the day after). Due to my stomach already feeling strange this made my nausea a whole lot worse. The whole day was spent either on the toilet or wondering when I would have to. We still managed to give John a good day and it was a nice peaceful relaxing day in that sense.

By the evening I was craving food badly but I managed to resist temptation as I knew that I would totally ruin any chances of getting answers for my current pain and symptoms. I went to bed early as although I drank lots of water I felt very lightheaded and dizzy.

I managed to sleep well all night somehow and in the morning I woke up feeling ok and luckily had no appetite. I drank more water and felt ok. I was slightly nervous with what they would find. I also had to do my Methotrexate injection which is my Crohn's and Arthritis treatment, and with the starvation and side effects of the injection, my nausea got worse as the morning went on. John took our children to school and we had organised for our son to go to a friend's after nursery and we had a few offers to help in case we were late to pick up our daughter. We arrived at hospital for the appointment but the wait to go through was very long, the nurses apologised for the long wait and said it was not normally like this. For me I knew what they were saying was true as I have had two colonoscopies previously and the wait was not as long as this one, however I finally went through and signed all consent forms and got undressed into the gown and waited on the bed. By this point I just wanted it over and done with. One of the nurses settled me in and explained she would try to put the canula in to save time for when I go through. I warned her that my veins were not great, and she calmly said "that's fine let's have a go". As she tried I was in slight pain but I knew I had to continue if I was to have sedation for the procedure. Unfortunately she was unable to do it properly and the needle was not quite in the right place. My poor hand was a little sore but it was all gauzed up and by the time I went through it was fine. The doctor and nurses explained what would happen as I went into theatre and the doctor who fortunately for me has performed a previous colonoscopy was here again and was one of the doctors from my Gastro department so I felt in safe hands. He managed first time to put a canula into my other hand and he said he would give me extra sedation plus some painkillers into it as the camera may slightly irritate my bowel due to having three previous operations. An oxygen tube was put in my nose to monitor my oxygen levels for the sedation and procedure. I felt a lot more disorientated this time round but was able to understand what the doctors and nurses were saying throughout. He said that he had to take some biopsies but overall the bowel looked ok and there was only a slight ulceration. He asked about my current symptoms and he hoped that I would recover soon and he felt that the symptoms may still be post operative problems and to be patient.

Once it was finished the oxygen tube was removed and I was taken back to the bay on the ward. As I was surprisingly alert afterwards I was able to have a drink and some biscuits immediately; and within no time at all because I felt ok, I was able to get dressed and wait for my reports, John was sent through and the nurse went through my report and also went through any side effects I may experience. I was given all of this on sheets too to take away with me.

Overall I left the hospital feeling ok. We drove straight to school to pick up both our children as our friend brought our son back to the school. We even went to the park afterwards to and I spoke to two of my friends. I was still feeling ok, so we also went to the shops so we could grab some evening snacks as both John and I had missed lunch all together as we left the hospital at 2:15 pm and arrived at 10:00 am.

We got home and I helped John with organising the laundry and sorting out dinner, but I had to stop half way through as I felt so weird. I felt sick and dizzy and had a headache. John gave me a drink of lucozade as an instant energy drink which helped and I had to lie on the sofa with my feet up as I felt quite ill. It was frustrating as now I was able to eat ironically I did not feel like eating but luckily I had a lot of wind which came up and this helped me manage to eat some dinner. It is normal to experience wind but I had not experienced this previously, however I did have extra sedation so maybe that is why.

John allowed me to rest the whole evening and I did not have to do a thing. He got the children ready for bed, read them stories and put them to bed, then had a DVD evening eating some snacks. I felt ok but still uneasy and dizzy. I spoke to my friend to say I should be ok for our practice walk the following morning, however when that morning arrived I felt really ill, as I had more normal side effects and would not manage the walk. A day of rest is what I did that morning. John said he would do the walk with me instead on another day. My procedure came at the right time as John had quite a long time off from holiday and rest days. So it was reassuring to know he was around to offer support and help with housework.

It took a long time after this colonoscopy to recover; I ended up phoning my IBD nurses and going to the doctors and I had severe stomach pain and very dark stools; I was told it was not due to the colonoscopy but there could be some problems with my upper stomach producing too much acid so I was advised to double up on my omeprazole (a drug given to help break down acid in stomach) and that an endoscopy (procedure where a camera goes down the throat to check the upper stomach) may need to be done to check my upper stomach is ok.

I was slightly scared but deep down knew that this may need to be done as I have had problems with acid reflux since diagnosis and also that I sometimes have trouble with swallowing foods and gag on certain foods; However it did not stop me complete a practice walk with John a week after the colonoscopy; it was actually a pleasant walk and the fresh air helped me.

The weekend of our charity walk arrived; we were staying with family and completed our walk in London. The whole day was great and the charity planned the event well. The kiddies enjoyed it too even though it rained. We completed the walk in about 2 hours as we had to stop for toilet breaks and due to rain it made us walk slower. I managed to meet up with some online "bowel buddies," from the support groups on Facebook. It was lovely catching up with them and seeing them in the flesh rather than on a computer screen. We had decided to do the charity walk yearly so that we could meet up annually for a catch up.

We received so much praise and support when we got home for completing the walk and we managed to raise over £300 for Crohn's and Colitis UK. I plan on doing some more fundraising events soon as it has given me the encouragement to do more and to know I had some support around me.

The walk really gave me motivation and although I struggled slightly with my stomach and joints on the day it was not like it has been in the past.

Since the walk I have had my Rheumatology appointment with the consultant and got told I was still possibly in remission as although my inflammation was slightly raised it was most likely due to the recent stomach upset I have had.

I also received a call from my Gastro consultant who gave me my biopsy colonoscopy results to say I was in remission with my Crohn's and that my pain and symptoms were most likely from IBS (Irritable Bowel Syndrome). So I am now waiting to be seen in clinic by him. This confirms what my dietician said last time regarding why I am struggling food wise. So I feel slightly closer to finding out why I am struggling with food right now. I felt so relieved that my Crohn's was not active.

I still needed to go to the doctors though as I had no idea now why I was so tired all the time, however when my GP checked my blood results she saw that quite anaemic and put me on some liquid iron as I was unable to take the tablet form. I also spoke to her about some strange headaches I have been having as they have occurred at the most unusual times and occur daily. I could be doing daily tasks and just bending down when these headaches appear and no painkillers help them. I told her I am reluctant to take too many and she agreed that I shouldn't and because I have had severe reactions to Amitriptyline in the past (November 2013 I blacked out in the car whilst on the lowest dose of them), so I was put on a similar drug called Toperimate.

Although this appointment made me feel quite fed up I was adamant to not let it all get to me. It's times like these appointments when I can slowly feel my gremlin try to make an appearance but somehow I manage to push them away. I am now slowly getting my life into control and accepting that this is just the way things are going to be. I'm now on a road again for the next few months on a trial and error with drugs, as I am unsure how these two medications will go as well as wondering what my Gastro consultant will prescribe for the IBS as well as what my dietician will decide to do next too. But however what I do know is that I am going to continue to battle this fight all the way. I look back at what has gone on in my life and feel strong I have succeeded so far, and if I have overcome that I can overcome this too.

Four

I have been on these two medications for a couple of days and feel so ill; feeling sick and having diarrhoea. I know it is nothing I have eaten as it normally causes constipation these days. I will be on the phone to my IBD nurses to discuss these symptoms and it may mean another doctor's appointment. People joke all the time with me that the doctors and hospital is my second home and I now just joke along with them. There is no shame in this fact, if it is what is going to make me well and keep me in remission then I would rather have endless appointments and be in remission, than endless appointments and being seriously ill. Regardless of being in remission or not these illnesses still need to be controlled regularly.

I ended up at the doctors because my IBD nurse helpline was not in use due to annual leave. However due to the doctor being a locum he was unable to help me properly and suggested reducing the amount of liquid iron I take and until my nausea has settled and to stay on the same dose of Toperimate. I was really frustrated as I knew this iron medicine was causing me to feel very ill. I decided to stop taking it all together and made another appointment with a different doctor the following week to get a second opinion.

I was glad I made this appointment as a few days later I felt really ill and was getting bad urgencies in needing to pass urine. So much so that I wet myself, this was so embarrassing but it happened alone and in the comfort of my own home. However it made me very worried. Over the next two days I was getting hot and cold flushes and back and side pain as well as pelvic pain when needing to pass urine. I decided to send a sample in but due to a change in their samples system, I was unable to do this, and instead had to fill a form in to leave with the doctor and to wait for a call back from a doctor; I never got this call, which was frustrating as it was on a Friday.

How I managed to get through the weekend I will never know and by the end of it, I felt bad but still had two days until my planned appointment. I ended up making it to my doctor's appointment and after doing another urine sample it showed slight traces of blood which confirmed I had a urine infection, so was put on antibiotics to treat my urine infection. I also discussed my acid reflux again and she suggested I take Lanzaprazole rather than Omeprazole as it is stronger and may relieve the acid reflux.

Things were going ok until a week later (which is now about a month after taking Toperimate) that I suffered from severe blurred vision; I was really worried and although at first I thought it was just the sunlight causing it, it appeared to get worse throughout the day; I managed to get an emergency appointment but the doctor I saw was unhelpful and did not want to listen to my concerns and symptoms, he felt that my blurred vision was the start of a migraine and told me that I should have been on a higher dose of Toperimate by now. I had no way of trying to explain why I was still on a low dose and he told me that increasing the Toperimate would help ease this. I did not feel completely happy but I had to trust in what he said, so that evening I took two tablets instead of one but immediately after I had stinging in my eyes and my vision was getting worse. I ended up calling out of hours and saw a doctor, (thanks to my parents for babysitting so late that night!). Although he could not see anything wrong at that appointment he said the symptoms sounded like Glaucoma and as a precaution I should go back to the GP first thing next morning and get a referral to an eye clinic.

I was feeling quite uneasy about it all. It felt strange not being able to see properly. I was dozing off unexpectedly too and I cannot really explain how I felt as I just didn't feel well and I was worried I would go blind. I've no idea why, but I normally trust my instincts, so I managed to get a GP appointment for the next morning and made sure that I saw a different doctor to the one I saw yesterday. The doctor looked concerned as soon as I sat down and explained my symptoms. My parents also checked the Toperimate effects and blurred vision was on the list so I mentioned this too. By the time I saw this doctor my vision was worse and I could not even see the largest letter on the eye test board. The doctor called the eye clinic for advice as well as getting me an appointment for the eye clinic at hospital that same day. He said the doctors at the eye clinic also felt it was a reaction to the Toperimate and that I should not take anymore. I was getting very concerned and luckily the day went quick enough for me to get some help from the hospital. We arranged for friends to have our children and for my parents to continue once they had finished work in case I was there a while.

I was at the hospital for a long time. I was seen quite quickly and as soon as the nurses and doctors did all of their examinations they looked very concerned and the amount of doctors coming into the room increased rapidly. I was told I had suffered a very rare side effect from the Toperimate and that I needed urgent treatment before the vision deteriorated further; I was warned that if I had not come today I would have been permanently blind as the condition I had was untreatable once it got to a certain point. I had so many scans and tests done on my eyes and they told me I had "Toperimate induced myopic shift and angle closure glaucoma". I was lucky that they managed to treat in time. I had endless scans on top of the normal ones as this was very rare and I was their second patient to ever have this so they needed all the research and evidence possible for their students and for future appointments. They gave me my treatment which was Atropine eye drops and I was told that I needed to remain at hospital for a further two hours until they were happy that my vision was returning to normal and that the pressure in my eyes was decreasing.

This was all very confusing as this is an area that I have no idea about and I have never had any issues with my eyes before. However the doctors at the hospital were so calm and patient and explained it all well through the use of drawings to explain what was happening to me.

Once they were happy with how my eyes were looking after treatment, I was able to go home but I needed to continue with treatment; I had to go back the following morning and by this appointment, from the scans and tests my eyes had returned to normal. They were amazed how quickly this happened and did further scans for their research and evidence. They showed me the scans from both days and I could not believe how closed up my eyes were and how they had managed to open completely after just one day of treatment. Even though things looked fine, I had to return after the weekend to check everything was still ok. I had to continue with the treatment over the weekend as a precaution. I was worried that my vision was still blurry even though my eyes had returned to normal and they explained to me that this was the side effect from my treatment and the drops they use during the scans and tests and nothing more.

By this point I was feeling angry at that first doctor I saw about my blurred vision. He implied that my blurred vision was a result of me choosing to not increase the Toperimate, when in fact it was actually the Toperimate that had caused it in the first place. I felt annoyed with myself that I actually trusted him and took that extra tablet as that may have ended up making my vision worse and could have caused permanent blindness. I ended up making an appointment with the GP practice manager to discuss my concerns as I felt he should have spent the time listening to me rather than assuming that I had caused the blurred vision myself. I had to wait a while to see the manager which was lucky really as it gave me time to see the eye clinic doctors again and by this point my vision was returning to normal and my eyes had completely reopened inside. As the clinic wanted to gather research and evidence of my rare side effect, I still had further tests and scans and was told to expect another two weeks for my vision to return to normal. Then I was able to stop the treatment and to return in two month's time to make sure that all was ok as my pupils were still much dilated so they wanted to make sure these returned back too.

I felt so relieved and thanked them all so much for what they had done. I asked to pass on my compliments to the doctor who initially alerted his team about my condition as he could have easily missed this and it was only because he did further tests to verify what he thought was happening that he found this rare Glaucoma in my eyes.

This taught me to be careful in future when trying new drugs and I think I will refuse further drugs similar to the Toperimate and Amitriptyline as I am unsure whether this could happen again.

It felt good a week later as my vision returned to normal and was quicker than what the hospital had said, however I then became ill again and had a severe sore throat and ear ache. I saw the doctor who referred me to the eye clinic and he was happy to see my eyes were better but was concerned about my high fever. He gave me antibiotics as my throat looked severely red and swollen and my ears were full of wax, so I had to use olive oil in them. He explained that this could be a side effect from the treatment as the drops need to escape somewhere.

I felt gutted and deflated that this was happening, but at the same time I felt grateful for having the treatment otherwise I could have been blind so I tried hard to keep remembering this. My gremlins tried to make an appearance but I did not allow them to come back. I pushed them out and carried on with daily tasks.

The antibiotics helped my throat but my ears were still very sore and the olive oil was not removing the wax. I went back to the doctors and I was told it was an ear infection so was given hydrocortisone ear drops that had a small amount of antibiotics in.

The endless doctor's visits were tiring but at least I felt they were coming to an end. I was also certain that this was all still to having the side effects from the Toperimate. My appointment with the practice manager had finally arrived and I explained my concerns and she also looked concerned. She said she would talk to the doctor in question and would write to me with a response as I said that I wanted to make a formal complaint. She also said that she would bring this up in their regular staff meetings. I said that I was glad this was happening as I was aware that the doctor who referred me to eye clinic was not happy and that this was an extremely near miss with my eyes that could have resulted in permanent blindness.

Although the outcome is probably not what I want (I feel that doctor should not be allowed to practice), I will have to patiently wait for the response and take it from there.

Looking back at this I still cannot believe that this would happen; I am in remission with both long term illnesses and yet I can still have something so drastic happen to me. I am no longer feeling happy with my body as I don't like the fact it reacts so badly. I am sure when you read this that you think I have just made all of this up for the story, but I can assure you all from my first book and this recent eye scare that this has all really happened; I have not written it just to make it seem more dramatic, this is a genuine account of what I've been through. This is why I am writing my story for you all to share as it really sounds like something you would see on a TV show. Like you as I am writing this as a diary I also have no idea what will happen next!

Five

After all this drama we now have the summer school holidays and when the holidays are over, my children will be all grown up; my little boy will be starting Reception class, which really does not seem possible as since he was born that is when my symptoms started so I have now spent the past four years with some form of illness. His milestones remind me of what I have overcome and I am pleased to say that although I have overcome many hurdles I am still here writing this book for you all. My little girl will also be starting Junior school and that also is quite scary. I am proud of her for taking her new challenge head on as she was worried about starting a new school but is now excited.

I have managed to plan a few trips each week throughout the summer holidays, which I am proud of as the past three years have been difficult. I don't have many hospital visits either so planning trips is so much easier. My fatigue has gone which I'm pleased about so it would appear that was also another side effect from the Toperimate.

I still get pains in the stomach when I need the toilet, however I have realised this is nothing compared to my recent eye scare and I am slowly accepting those pains are going to be a part of me for some time.

It's reassuring to be able to start to write some positive things about my life, I am over the moon knowing we have some exciting days out soon. We have already been to the seaside, park and visits to the city and family visits. My symptoms and illnesses have not made it that easy for me to enjoy. The heat makes me very tired and it is a slight reminder of what I have and that although I feel ok I still need to take it easy and not over exert myself. Again the gremlin could quite easily appear but I think that I have accepted these little things are with me forever, the gremlin has decided to give in and not bother anymore.

All this time I thought the gremlin was there to punish me but it was really there for me to learn how to accept myself. I can now be grateful for those gremlins as it has taught me a valuable part of life and alongside my special friend M I have become a more positive person.

I no longer worry about what could happen anymore, but I will trust my instincts if I feel something is wrong. I had an instinct that my eyes were not right and that I could possibly go blind which I nearly did, so I definitely need to keep control of my gut instinct and not allow them to turn me into a worrier I have been in the past. It is strange to explain how to do this, but as time goes on I have learnt how to place things in my mind so that I can carry on with life. Don't get me wrong, I struggle daily with the simple things but I no longer worry and just forget about what I have not done and praise myself for what I have achieved even if it is just getting up, making the meals and getting children ready. My house is more of a mess these days now and I worry less but I know that the queen will never visit me and that if people want to judge me for what my house looks like then I am not interested in them. We all can only do our best each day, others manage more or less than me but who cares; and I am not in any competition with anyone.

We have another five weeks to go of the holidays, and as I said so many trips to look forward to! However the trauma from my eye scare has finally appeared and the fatigue has returned. My stomach is very bloated which I am sure is caused from my body being stressed with all of the antibiotic eye drops and ear drops that I have put inside me. It is days like these where I could easily fall back into depression, however having an idea of the cause of my fatigue and bloatiness has helped slightly. I can feel the gremlin trying to force its way through but once again I am not letting it win. It is a constant fight daily, not just with my health but surviving and getting through the days, I keep thinking about the trips we have planned over the holidays which helps to beat the gremlins.

Six

It is now a good two weeks on from my eye scare and I am still not feeling very well. My ear infection is still there and I am now getting pain in my sides again alongside smelly and orange coloured urine. I met with the Practise Manager to discuss my complaint and have also had a response from the doctor in question. However I was very unhappy and upset by his response as he took no responsibility for any of his actions and it seemed as if he felt I was lying about what other doctors had told me to do with regards to the Toperimate on previous visits to the doctors before the blurred vision occurred, which led to me writing a very long letter to the Practise Manager and have also started to look into solicitors to take this further. My mum has spoken to some of the doctors at where she works and they are disgusted by what happened to me and said that I should not have been put on Toperimate in the first place because of the long list of side effects and that it should only be used for severe epilepsy. I have no idea where the complaint will end up but what I do know is that since my complaint and eye scare I am now having panic attacks just before having appointments in the GP surgery. I am losing my trust in some of them now and I feel that I will be treated differently due to my recent complaint. I feel like I am in a dilemma as I would love to just not go as often to the doctors but having two chronic lifelong illnesses which need constant monitoring, I have to attend regularly as well as have monthly blood tests.

I have made two long lists for my GP and my Gastroenterologist. I also feel that my panic attacks are a new way of the gremlin trying to appear as well as my recent trauma. I do feel quite depressed again and have isolated myself on social media as well as with my friends because I feel like I need to step back and re-evaluate my life and what is happening on my own. I had to make some difficult decisions on social media but glad I did it as I am hoping it will help ease the stress and I hopefully will not let things said on social media such as Facebook bother me from now on.

My next appointment is with my GP and I need to talk to her about my urine problems and pain in my sides; I have already seen a doctor about this just after my eye scare and he said it was a possible prolonged side effect and could possibly be kidney stones; so I should return if it persists which is why I am attending as well as needing more Lanzaprazole and to discuss my fatigue and headaches again.

After this appointment I have three hospital appointments; the first with my Rheumatology nurses, and I am relieved this appointment is getting closer as my joints are painful again.

My next appointment is with my Gastroenterologist, and I need to discuss my recent reluctance of trying new drugs and to also explain what the dietician has advised as well as to check that the other drugs that I am on are ok to be on long term. I also need to discuss my stomach as it is still very descended and lumpy and also hurts in places and feels very hard.

As you may see, having a chronic illness or more than one can be so unpredictable; I have never known life to be so up and down. However for once in my life I have come to accept that this is just the way my life will be from now on and that without my illnesses life would probably be quite boring. As much as I would like a cure as I don't really want these in my life forever; I have come to realise that I need to make the best of this horrible situation and as much as the gremlin tries to appear, (like it is right now as I write this), I am somehow being strong and fighting it away.

Rather than go on about my health, I am going to switch and talk about the summer holidays and how that although I have all of this going on we have managed to have some good trips out. We have visited family; we visited a zoo and also went to the seaside and swimming pool. We have had picnics at the park and been to the library too. I also took them on my own shopping in Norwich city and treated them to lunch. These have all been big achievements and I am so proud that I have managed to do these trips still.

I also met up with M and ended up having an indoor picnic at my house. Our children loved it and we watched an old dance show DVD as M's daughter also attends the same dance school. As I've said earlier, whenever I see M we always managed to continue our conversations from where we left off; and I feel so comfortable talking to her about anything as I know that she will support and listen without judging or criticising me.

We have also been out for a meal and went to the cinema in the city; this was a lovely family day out. We also went back to the seaside and visited the sea life centre. With family we went on a trip to the dinosaur park, this is our yearly trip with my cousin and her children, it is such a fun day out.

As well as trips out, my daughter has also managed to have a couple of play days with her friends. Due to my son being ill with ear infections during the holidays it was hard to plan a play day for him, however towards the end of the holidays he had a friend over to play as I did not want him to feel left out.

We managed to do a lot with our children this year as the past few years have been even more up and down than this year and although we still had to squeeze in various appointments in amongst our trips, we survived the holidays. I ended up with a second urine infection which made me feel quite poorly; I ended up on my third lot of antibiotics.

It can get quite frustrating as I like to plan well in advance for our trips out but every week, inevitably something unpredictable happens. I did fall back into depression again as all of these appointments were getting quite tedious and because of the after effects of my decisions of leaving social media, things felt quite rotten. Friends ended up being offended by my decisions to limit my "friends list" and I felt like whatever I chose to do I was always in the wrong. The doctors were making me feel guilty for complaining and my friends were making me feel guilty for leaving social media and didn't understand the way that I did it. My life with Crohn's is already difficult with feeling judged and there are days where I already feel like no one understands me.

Seven

I am now getting to the end of my third lot of antibiotics and I have not noticed much improvement as the pain in my back and sides are still there as well as it now getting a stinging sensation as I pass urine, as well as developing a strange spotty rash. On top of this, my son still has a gunky ear and although the antibiotics did work as it has stopped the ear from leaking discharge, the inside of his ear still looks sore and contains lots of discharge, so we both have appointments with the GP again.

But before this I had my Rheumatology appointment with the nurses. I explained about my joints hurting lots and told her about all of my infections and my reaction to the Toperimate. She checked my joints and was mainly concerned about my shoulder which has recently started to suffer too. She said that she felt it was a result of the drugs I was taking and all of my infections that I have had so did not want to alter my treatments at present, however she said that if it does not settle down I would need to phone them and then they will arrange for me to be seen again. I would then be given steroid injections and my Methotrexate injections dosage would be increased.

It is now a wait for the following week to have my Gastroenterology appointment regarding my Crohn's. I have no idea what he will say but I have my long list of questions waiting for him as per usual.

We are towards the end of the summer holidays and the children are starting to get bored. We had run out of money for any more trips out so we were back to looking at things we can do at home, such as play dough, making biscuits and cakes and doing painting. John and I took them swimming once more and we had days planned with family. Even with all mine and my son's appointments we managed to get out to get the last of their school uniform, it was shoe fitting time but luckily I booked an appointment so this trip was less stressful. I managed to get them all of their shoes and clothes that they needed on my own. My parents helped too in finding some uniform on their trips too which helped immensely.

My appointment with my Gastroenterologist went ok, my Crohn's is still in remission and my IBS seems to be calming down, however he was concerned about my joints and my stomach issues with the reflux. He decided to let my Rheumatology nurses decide how to best treat my joints but prescribed me some Ranitidine to use alongside the Lanzaprazole for my stomach problems and reflux as my stools were constantly changing colour and sometimes were very dark, as well as the pain I was experiencing and the amount of acid I was getting in my throat. He decided though that if the drug did not improve my problems within a month of taking them that he would arrange an endoscopy as my stomach is the only part of the body I have not had checked since diagnosis. I felt relieved that things were looking more positive and hoped the drug helped me.

My GP appointment had arrived. After a couple of appointments I am now back on some more antibiotics as although my urine samples are clear there may be some irritation still in the bladder causing my pain and discomfort, however if things don't settle I need to go back and be referred for an ultrasound and to see a specialist. My ears have finally been cleared of infection however they need syringing now. My rash is also a viral rash. During this my joints have been worse than ever, so I called my Rheumatology nurses but they have decided that due to my levels returning back to normal since my last appointment with them that they feel my joints are flaring from my infections but if things do not settle again after this 4th lot of antibiotics to call them again. I also have received another letter back regarding my complaint and the surgery is not going to take my complaint further so, in other words, if I want to, I should take it further on my own. I decided that because the complaint procedures were causing me stress and upset that I would leave it for now and maybe take it further once my joints and infections settle down.

I am feeling more and more exhausted each day and I am sure it is due to all of the infections, and I keep hoping that things will get easier. But as you can see when things do look brighter and ok, they are only for short spells at a time which is very frustrating, and not just for me but for my family also. Although I feel happier and more positive this time round, my life is still as unpredictable as ever. I can still see the light at the end of the tunnel so I feel reassured there, my gremlins are not causing me any problems, but I do have some very down days.

I have returned to social media for support as I could not cope on my own; I would love to be able to; but I desperately need my internet buddies for advice as a result of deciding to keep my Facebook friend's list to a minimum, I seem to have lost a lot of friends. I don't keep in contact with many people now outside of the internet so I am relying on some of my Facebook friends for comfort. It sounds very one sided but I know they rely on me just as much as I do on them. I hope one day we can meet up as we offer each other a huge deal of invaluable support.

<u>Eight</u>

We are now in September 2014 and it's that time when the children go back to school, a couple of days before they went back were hard. My joints were so stiff and achy that doing daily chores and housework was hard. My viral rash was very itchy and it started to look horrible now that it had spread all over my body. I felt weak and not my normal bright self. I noticed my eldest was becoming very irritable and argued a lot with me. Somehow I managed to find the energy to sit with her and listen to her worries and troubles; I am not sure how much she is worrying but she has said she feels left out. I felt horrible for making her feel this way. It is difficult to give her time when my son takes a lot of it up, either with his behavioural problems or dealing with his medications for his Asthma, Eczema and ears. I decided that on the days John is home I will try and spend more time with her once our son is in bed, doing girly things like colouring and Hama beads and loom bands.

They have been back at school for a week and two days and we are all tired. My son is finding it hardest of all as it is also that time when the seasons change so his Asthma is flaring. He is relying on his pumps a lot right now. His Eczema is looking better apart from his nail still looks very weird, from where his Eczema around his finger looks very red and scaly.

My joints are still horrible, but after speaking to the nurses again I have now been given an urgent appointment at hospital to see them. I have been experiencing a lot of diarrhoea and stomach cramps and ended up at the doctors again, I was told it is a reaction to the amount of antibiotics I have been on, She also examined my back and diagnosed it as joint inflammation by looking at the position of where the pain occurs.

Most recently I am experiencing stomach pains quite high up in the stomach. My initial feeling is Gallstones but it could be the stomach acid problems. I see my GP soon as I thought it best to keep them updated with what my hospital nurses and doctors have said. Especially as I have been seeing various doctors at the GP surgery over the past month, I also felt that it was best even though I am losing faith in some of them that I should see my regular GP for consistency.

My daughter gets more special time with me now so she doesn't feel left out now. She loves her new Junior school and seems to enjoy it. They are both thriving and enjoying their extra responsibilities. They are both very independent which is good for me especially whilst I am struggling with my joints.

The only main issue I am struggling with is this gremlin. It seems to have appeared out of nowhere. I have started getting suicidal thoughts again. I am feeling really lonely especially now I have isolated myself from people. It was definitely needed but I feel as if I have lost even more friends now because of it. I have no idea if anyone is gossiping about me and spreading rumours but it certainly feels like it as not many people now will talk to me at school; all because of social media. It has proved to me though that I did the right thing as they have taken my actions the wrong way and it shows how social media can make people interpret things the wrong way or the opposite way to what people actually mean. I have a few friends still who are talking to me but our lives are so busy. I don't have much time anymore when doing the school runs as I have to rush around to get them both to school, and then with doctors appointments after school and their additional activities after school, we don't have a lot of time after school either for time to catch up.

This gremlin appears at night now and is keeping me awake and I dreamt of ways to harm myself. I managed to stop myself from following this through as I kept thinking of my children. I felt horrible that I have allowed these thoughts back into my mind. However these thoughts are just like my two illnesses; they are so unpredictable and I never know when they will appear.

I am hoping that these thoughts are just a temporary thing as the thought of it being long term like it has been in the past frightens me. I am also hoping that it is occurring as I have been feeling unwell recently, I have started to lose weight, feeling nauseous and starting new drugs, I have a feeling this is just part of my new anxiety with my panic attacks.

As I've said many times already in this book, these feelings do feel different and only feel dream-like and not as much of a reality like they have felt in the past. You may wonder how I can tell the difference, but this time round I was actually dreaming of self harming whereas in the past I have been awake and thought up ways myself of self harming. There is definitely a difference and I am happy that I have recognised this by myself as there are times I feel insane but having that recognition is making me realise that I am not insane and I am able to change these dreams into more positive ones.

Nine

I have had a really bad week, I saw my GP regarding my stomach pain, and she thought the same as me, it was my Gallstones, she checked through all my records and saw that the scan I had during 2012 confirmed I had them. She felt surgery was my best option even though she did not want me to go through more, she decided to write to my Crohn's consultant to see if they could request the scans through them as it would be quicker than doing a whole new referral. I needed urgent blood tests the same day to see if Gallstones were noticeable in the blood tests. I filled her in with what my consultant said as well as the Rheumatology nurses needing to see me the following day as my joints are bad, so I had extra blood tests for the nurses to detect inflammation. I came out with mixed feelings; I felt relieved that my GP listened to me and is actually doing something about my problems. And I also felt sad that it's very likely it will mean more surgery. This would mean my fourth operation in two years.

The following day I had my Rheumatology nurse appointment and after a thorough examination, as well as getting a detailed history of all my medication and history, she decided to get some advice from the registrars. Due to having severe pain in back, shoulders, knees as well as my hands, the registrar felt it was best to book a scan on my hands to see if anything is going on as it's hard to tell from feeling my joints and looking at blood test results because of the type of arthritis that I have. They also decided to test and scan for Spondylitis of the spine as my symptoms fitted it quite well. I came away again feeling relieved and scared but I did not even think of asking more about Spondylitis so when I got home I checked out the Arthritis UK webpage and read all the information on it. It definitely sounded like me when going through all the symptoms. I didn't really check out the treatment as I did not want to depress myself in case it was not great.

So now I am back to two years ago, maybe not with such a severe diagnosis, but back to the endless appointments, hospital scans and tests to find out what is going on and preparation for another operation. I am fortunate enough to have some friends and family who have been great in listening to my problems, and also my mother in law has offered again to come down and help me either whilst I have more surgery or if my joints get so bad that I need help.

I feel sad knowing and feeling my joints are deteriorating day by day, even washing up; writing and opening the kiddies' school drink bottles are causing me extreme pain. I have been advised to take the maximum dose of painkillers daily now, which takes the pain slightly away but not completely.

John has been great too and allowing me to rest as much as possible, however I am trying to still do things every day to keep myself sane and to not feel like a burden. I am still doing the school walks and I'm determined to continue for as long as I can. I had to cancel my voluntary work due to hospital appointment and my joints hurting too much to do it.

Our children are coping well but I have not told them about any of this yet as I still have no idea what will really happen, but I will know when the time is right to talk to them about it all. Once I know what will happen then I can work out a plan so that they know and have the reassurance of who will look after them during my appointments and possible surgery.

A week later and I feel unwell; I'm hardly eating because I get a lot of stomach pain a few hours after eating so it puts me off. I'm also getting a lot of acid build up still, even whilst taking my extra drug. I keep getting low fevers and also having quite bad shivering attacks, my joints are still hurting especially in my lower back and shoulders.   My Crohn's is flaring occasionally, as my bowel movements are all over the place again, it is starting to get confusing as to what is what anymore and what is causing what symptom that I feel a bit in limbo, until I've had my tests and scans anyway. I am back to my GP soon so I will hopefully find out what is happening with regards to my ultrasound for the Gallstones.

I also had to make a difficult and upsetting decision and I let the school know I was unable to do voluntary work this half term. I feel awful and sad that I just don't feel well enough to help them. I feel a failure and feel very weak that I cannot find the inner strength to plough through the work regardless of my problems. Of course this is just my feelings, the school have been very understanding, however for me I feel this is not going to help me get a job in the future as it is just more proof for future employers that I would be a burden to them and that I would be too unreliable.

The time came for me to return to my GP, and she had not heard from my consultant so decided to do her own referral for me to have some ultrasounds on my upper stomach regarding my Gallstones. However she did say due to my complex health issues she will be seeking advice on who should operate on me. I still had my red spotty rash and she diagnosed this as Psoriasis. So I have some steroid and moisturising cream to apply. I also noticed that I had a large lump appear on right side of stomach near all my pervious surgery scars. She said this was a Hernia but due to having a lot going on this will have to take a backseat for a little while.

I had my monthly blood tests with the additional Spondylitis ones. I still have not heard about my scans on my hands, so I contacted my rheumy nurses who told me my bloods showed I don't have spondylitis and that I should receive an appointment in the next few weeks. I am waiting to hear from them again as I need to know what happens next as I still get bad back and shoulder pains.

My Gallstone and Hernia pain is causing me more discomfort than normal right now, however I am not allowing it to ruin my everyday life; I went out with two friends and had lunch out together, it was lovely spending the day with them, we all needed it so it was good to get away.

Certain people are still ignoring me, but I am now trying my best to ignore it all, it's hard as I don't like the feelings that go through my head sometimes, however I keep telling myself that I have too much going on health wise to be worried about other people.

I am trying to lower my expectations of others and to concentrate on the ones who do care and talk to me and not focus on the ones who obviously have no further interest in me. The reason I am struggling so much with this is the fact I don't really know what has happened and they have never made it clear as to why they are ignoring me.

Ten

So the waiting game starts again, still waiting for my Gallstone ultrasound, as well as the scans on my joints. I am the type of person who likes to know what is happening and this is very much out of my comfort zone.

I finally received my letter for my appointment and the week waiting for it to arrive was so long. Whilst waiting for this scan, I ended up being in a lot of pain when going to the toilet, so much so that I nearly passed out; A couple of days later I was getting a lot of pelvic pain and discomfort and my urine was red/orange in colour and very smelly. I ended up going to out of hours and they confirmed I had another urine infection so was put on some more antibiotics. I was concerned with how many I have had in such a short space of time, so I called my regular GP, and she reassured me that my kidneys will be scanned in my ultrasound and that I should arrange and book an appointment with her for when the results are back so that she can give me a more accurate and informed answer.

I finally felt my health was finally getting the attention it needs and deserves; and I'm finally getting my trust back with the GP's.

My ultrasound scan appointment arrived, and I was not in there long, and he advised me to see my GP in a week's time for the results. He did not give me much information out about what he had found, so I was anxiously waiting to see my GP. Within this time I also heard from my rheumatology nurse who gave me some good news that I do not have the Spondylitis gene. I felt relieved but yet again I was back to square one with working out where all my joint pain was from.

Before I went to see my GP for my results I ended up back at the doctors and out of hours twice with two more urine infections. I was advised to let my regular GP know in case further investigations needed to take place as to why I was getting so many. I ended up on further antibiotics to hopefully settle the infections.

Although I felt so tired from all these symptoms, I was still continuing to not let it all get to me. Even friends from the children's schools had commented on how happy I looked regardless of what was going on. I was receiving so much support from a select few friends and it felt good to know that I still had some friends who care for me as much as I care for them.

A week had gone by, and it was the time to get my ultrasound results, I was feeling quite scared with what she was going to tell me. However she didn't tell me anything that I didn't already know. The scan confirmed that I still had Gallstones and she felt it was best to have surgery to remove them, so she will be referring to general surgery as well as writing to my Gastroenterologist to inform him. She advised me to also ring the IBD nurses to explain the Ranitidine is not helping the stomach acid and reflux issues, she said it will possibly mean an endoscopy to rule out any other problems that are causing this and she also prescribed an additional drug called Metaclopramide to help with the extra pain and discomfort the Gallstones and acid reflux are causing me. However this drug is for short term use only so I can only take for two weeks. I also need to continue with the steroid cream to resolve the Psoriasis as the spots are still very red. She also has put an alert on my file so that if I have any more urine infections then samples and referrals need to be done.

It is now yet again a waiting game for referrals. I also have my ultrasound on my hands to see what is causing my hand joint pain.

It was time for me and my son to have our flu jabs also, Due to my Methotrexate injections, it was not safe for us to have the live vaccines as it could make me seriously unwell and I could end up in hospital needing additional treatments, so we both had to have an injection, however on arrival, I was told that I could not have mine due to my infections and because I was on antibiotics, so I now have to rebook mine for a week after I finish my fortnightly course of antibiotics. So my poor boy had to have his on his own, he was very brave, and I felt bad as he had to go through pain due to my illness and drugs. I really wish he could have had the nasal spray instead as it would have been pain free for him, but it would not have been safe for me. I felt selfish, but in some circumstances I don't feel I have much choice. Luckily it's all done with now and I know we are not alone in having to do this, so many other children go through the same and worse so it helped me to come to terms with it, it's just a shame he is so young and does not understand, but some extra treats and cuddles seemed to help him!

Eleven

The waiting is the most difficult of all, as you have even less control of anything. Luckily the Metaclopramide has been helping with my stomach symptoms but I'm still not sleeping properly and the pain can still get intense at times. My Hernia is even more noticeable, I suppose this is due to losing weight and so my stomach is less bloated which means my Hernia is poking out of my stomach more.

In the media as well lately there has been some sad news of a well known celebrity called Lynda Bellingham who died of colon cancer. It has touched me in a more personal way as her story sounds very similar to mine but I have Crohns rather than cancer. Her honest interview on TV before she passed was hard to watch as her experiences and feelings of those were so like mine. It also brought back a lot of memories with my friend M who is going through a similar cancer battle herself. Lynda reminded me of M as their positive outlooks and their views on life are very alike, and my outlook is very similar too nowadays.

It has been extra hard as I seem to know of a few people suffering with cancer all around me right now; I suppose being part of support groups and having chronic illnesses myself that this was inevitable. I suppose that this is where I am still quite naive of certain issues and just assume that I and people around me will never suffer anything so horrid, but in reality this is untrue. These sorts of health issues are more common than you first expect. It makes me feel grateful for the life I have and even more grateful in managing to overcome my two life saving operations in 2012. Anyway, as M would say, life must go on and we must grab each day as if it is our last! And as I say to people onwards and upwards is the only way to go in life!

So as I said, the waiting game continues for me, however I have another ultrasound next week on my hands, which is needed now, even as a type right now, my hands are screaming in pain, but I carry on regardless. My joints all over my body are so sore and I either feel like I am carrying so many bags on my back or that I am just ninety-three, and not thirty-three years old. I am still continuing to take my antibiotics for my last urine infection, but I am slightly worried about having less control of my bladder.

Whilst waiting for referrals and appointments I managed to keep myself occupied in a different way at the doctor's surgery. I was asked to participate in a student discussion with their medical students as part of their training. It lasted forty-five minutes and I found it very therapeutic and I found it most helpful for me as well as managing to help them too. They asked me so many various questions regarding my health as a child, as well as what my health was/ is like pre- Crohns and post Crohns. You could tell the students were shocked as to how much has happened to me, but at the same time, they were full of empathy and asked very personal questions about my feelings of certain aspects, which I found reassuring as I have never really been asked by medical doctors how I feel about things, it is mainly concentrating on my physical symptoms. I thoroughly enjoyed those forty-five minutes and I feel I have been given a chance to help future GP's recognise early signs of my illnesses which I hope will be able to help people in the future receive quicker diagnosis and treatment.

A couple of weeks on and we are now in October, and I have finally finished my last course of antibiotics, however there is a bottle of cranberry juice in the fridge just in case it re-occurs, I am waiting for my flu jab, so I cannot have any more antibiotics, well at least until after the vaccine. I have also had my ultrasound on my wrists, I am unsure how this went as he did not say a lot, so I will wait until the report has been sent to Rheumatology and will try and be patient until my next Rheumatology appointment next year. I ended up calling my specialist IBD nurses again, who confirmed that my endoscopy would be soon and I have an extra appointment with my Gastroenterolgist in December, which I assume is to get results of the endoscopy or to discuss my Gallstone and acid problems, I was advised to call his secretary to confirm the reason for the appointment, but still not heard anything, I have another appointment with my GP soon too as she said she will just refer to the surgeons if we have both had no response by the time I see her. It is so frustrating but at least my GP is on my side now, and I don't feel like this is all in my head, I am finally feeling reassured that my GP has my best interests at heart.

The children have had a week off school for half term, and we managed to do a couple of things with them, such as take them swimming, we also had a trip to the seaside and had dinner at a nice fish and chip shop along the sea front. I also plan to take the children trick or treating, this activity is draining and exhausting me just thinking about it, as the half term week has not been a great one for me as my stomach has been hurting badly; and I just feel generally unwell.

John has just started his long run of work days, 7 to be precise, and they are long days too, It's not going to be the best of weeks, but at the end of it John gets 5 days at home, and two of those days we will be out spending time just the two of us in our old town of Romford seeing some friends. My parents are going to have the children overnight and it is a relief knowing John and I have some time together on our own as we really need it.

From the outside people may think we have it all, but there is one thing in our relationship that is still nonexistent and it burdens me with guilt all the time; our sex life has disappeared and I really hoped I would find the strength and courage to get this part of our life back on track; John is great but I feel scared as I have no idea how much longer he will be able to cope with this. I have learnt the best I can to deal with it all, but for John who hardly says how he feels, who knows?

I feel like I am having to force myself and try my hardest to focus on this part of our relationship, but like everything, my health and appointments and fatigue kind of take over all the time.

Twelve

Well those 7 days went really fast but I struggled during that time, especially as I ended up with severe lower back pain, resulting in me going to the doctors, and was given some heat gel to try, however after three days the pain is returning again, so I am unsure what the cause of the pain is. I also had my daughter off sick with headaches and vomiting, but when taking her to the doctors they felt the sickness was due to her headaches, she has headaches before so we are now back to keeping headaches diaries for her and to return in a few weeks time. My son has also been having some rashes and some more personal and private issues which I will not disclose as this book is about my health not anyone else's. The weather has turned a lot colder too so my joints are quite bad. Within this time, I have also received an appointment for my Gastroscopy which is another term for endoscopy (camera down the throat procedure). I am so scared that I already feel quite panicky about it, I suppose it's the fear of the unknown as I have never had this procedure before only colonoscopies, and due to my acid reflux I gag anyway so I have no idea how I will manage but needs must to find out what's happening as symptoms are still bizarre. Now I have two appointments at the hospital in one week, both requiring help from people with childcare and help in getting children from school. This is when I feel most grateful for my parents because on these occasions I am unsure of whether my friends could help so my parents are taking time off work to help.

This is the most perfect time to talk a little bit about my relationship with my mum in particular, I mean both my mum and dad have been great and they are both my best friends, however my mum is more than just a mum, she is my best friend, my sister, my soul mate and my guardian angel. We have a very special close relationship that nobody could ever come between; she is also there to listen to me and vice versa, however over the past two years it has been more her listening to me, but she does not seem to mind, and I feel she is the perfect role model of what a mum should be like and I hope my daughter and I can have a similar relationship as she gets older. I really admire her work ethic and she is always there for others before herself, I know I share most of her qualities and I hope my daughter will share them too.

My mum and I have managed to overcome quite a lot of hurdles and I believe that this is because we always stick together as a family and it really does help when dealing with struggles to have that closeness and uniqueness to manage any problem in life. Don't get me wrong no family is perfect but I certainly would not change anything about mine, I love them all dearly even extended family and I feel lucky to have them.

I also have a very good second family which is John's family and with some in particular I am able to talk about my health and they are all very supportive, caring and understanding that it makes me feel lucky again to have found them. John and I have known each other sixteen years and so his family feels like an extension of my own.

I know many out there do not have what I have, but I do feel that having the family who I have around me has helped immensely shape me into the person I am now and with all the support and understanding I get from my families; it has

45

helped me carry on and to stay positive in life and has given me something to live for.

Thirteen

So back to the story and another two to three weeks have gone by, and it's getting closer to my Gastroscopy and Gastroenterology appointment. I had to go back to my GP regarding following up on my Gallstones. She has decided to refer me to my previous surgeon as he also performs laparoscopies (surgery done via key-hole surgery, which is less evasive that open surgery), so she is hoping as he knows me he would be able to perform this operation to remove my Gallbladder, she also decided to do this as a matter of urgency, which scared me but she explained that it is mainly due to my medical history, and I then spoke about my bowel issues and she felt they were all related to the Gallstones and acid reflux problems I am getting. She also mentioned my Hernia but we are unsure if anything will be done at this stage.

I felt relieved but scared as things are slowly getting closer to happening now; as well as finally having my GP on my side and acting quickly on my symptoms. I have now been taken off Metcolpramide and put on Buscopan as my symptoms were no better so it was safer to try the Buscopan for a while whilst waiting for appointments.

Life is slightly topsy-turvy at the moment as I have a few issues with the children too; my son is on antibiotics again and he reacts strangely whilst on them, and my daughter seems to be coming home upset and has informed me of some worrying situations between two girls in her year group. I have finally spoken to the teacher who will try and talk to the two children and deal with it on my daughter's behalf. My daughter is also lucky enough to have some very supportive friends who are watching out for her. However once again I am feeling "why me and us?" Everything always seems to happen at once. My daughter is using her worry tree a bit more now so I felt this was the time to talk to her about the possibility of having another operation. She took it well and seemed to understand what was happening, I gave her a lot of mummy-time, cuddles and reassurance which seems to have helped, as her only worries right now are what's happening at school with the two girls.

I am trying to keep my mind occupied so I can forget about all these issues and try to forget about the current pain I am in (stomach pains on and off, occasional diarrhoea and bloating, stomach and bowel spasms). I have managed to do this by organising a fundraiser event to raise money for Crohn's and Colitis UK (I told you in book one to look out for further fundraising events!). I am overwhelmed with how much support I have had from friends at the schools. I have even managed to ask local businesses for raffle prize donations and most have been able to help me. I have really enjoyed organising it and I now just hope the actual day goes to plan. My children will be baking cakes to sell, and I have managed to create some prizes from items at home, as well as bake my speciality Christmas cake as the event is around Christmas time. I am enjoying this side of things and I hope that by doing this it will keep me positive for the few weeks ahead with my appointments and gastroscopy.

Fourteen

Well although some parts were positive I ended up back at the doctors. It was due to over the weekend having another urine infection, however this one was much scarier as it was pure red urine in the toilet. It scared me so I phoned the NHS advice line and went to an out of hour's appointment who confirmed I had an infection and was put on another course of antibiotics. I have had so many in the past few months I went back to the GP and she was very concerned. I was put on a low dose of antibiotics to take once a night as a preventative, but she also discussed that she will speak to my regular GP about being referred to Urology. I was warned the tests during this referral would not be pleasant, but I said to the GP that at this point I did not care as I was getting more poorly each time I had an infection and they were draining me.

I came away feeling deflated again as although I want to know what is wrong, the appointments and referrals are becoming never ending. I feel like they should give me a totally new body and then I may be able to get on with my life and do the things I want to be doing, such as working, and spending proper time with the children without feeling tired and ill all the time.

The only thing that kept me going that week was my fundraiser event, and it was a big success. John and I raised just over £135 and that was also thanks to friends and local businesses who donated. I also had about fourteen people attend the event and bought raffle tickets and cakes as well as ordering at the cooking show. A friend who has her own business making jewellery sold her products. The sales from both the cooking show and the jewellery stall gave the charity a percentage of them. I felt so happy, knowing that the event went well and the hard work was well worth it and paid off. It also felt good knowing that I have some friends who are caring, thoughtful and offer great support and encouragement.

It feels strange and empty now the event is over so I am now concentrating on Christmas. This is the first Christmas since our son was born where I feel ok. I am still in pain and still have some symptoms and although I have a lot of things health wise going on, they are all more minor issues and not as serious as before. So I am trying to make the most of this and plan a lovely Christmas for the family. Our financial worries are continuing but at least my ESA (Employment Support Allowance) is here to stay so it has allowed me to get the children most of what they want for Christmas. This year we will be spending Christmas day at my parents and then like normal spending boxing day with John's parents. I love Christmas as I love giving my friends and family their presents; I love seeing the smiles on their faces as they open the presents. That is what is most important the giving, not the receiving!

The past few weeks since my fundraiser event have been hectic. I've managed to complete all my Christmas present shopping, got my parcels and cards that needed sending posted, as well as write all my cards out. I did this mainly because my gastroscopy was drawing close and I was really unsure what they would find and for some reason concerned as to whether I would end up in hospital. The fear is mainly from two years ago spending half of December in hospital, and I wanted to ensure I had everything in place at home in case the same happened again. I wanted to make it as easy for John to complete the deeds if this again had happened.

I had to starve the night of my Gastroscopy which was fine as by this point I was losing my appetite and getting severe pains in my throat and stomach. At one point there was not one part of my body that didn't hurt. I also had weird coloured stools and diarrhoea so I sent a stool sample off for the labs to test.

The day of the procedure was here and I was very scared as I had never had this particular procedure before, but as soon as I saw some familiar nurses in the unit I felt relieved. I was called in to get my blood pressure taken and to talk through the forms and procedures and sign all consent forms. The nurse explained what would happen and I felt more with ease at what was coming. However there was a long wait until I had been called in again. The waiting was hard as I had just wanted to get it all done with. I was finally called through and was sent straight to the theatre room. The nurses and doctors were excellent and the worst part was when the doctor had to put the canula in as it took two attempts for me to be sedated; I don't really remember much else apart from being wheeled out onto a recovery ward where the nurses monitored me and it did not take me long to come round from the sedation. I was allowed a drink and some biscuits and then waited for a nurse to explain my results and escort me back to John. The nurse explained that they had found a Hiatus Hernia in my oesophagus/ stomach, so I was advised to eat smaller meals and to try not to eat after 6 pm as this would relieve my symptoms. The nurse also explained my results to John too.

For the next twenty-four hours John needed to stay with me at home until the sedation had fully worn off, and just as well as I did feel quite queasy and drowsy for a day or so after, my throat was very sore so I stuck to soft mushy foods for the first few days.

It was only four days later after the procedure I was back at the hospital to get my results from the consultant. My biopsy results from the Gastroscopy and my stool sample were not back but he said that due to how small my Hiatus Hernia was he felt that my symptoms were caused by the Gallstones and he said he would speak with the surgeon to speed up my appointment as he felt the surgery needed to happen as soon as possible because my symptoms were affecting me so badly. This was the point where I could hardly eat any food; I sometimes struggled to swallow and the acid reflux was bad at night and during the day. My mouth fills up with burning acid and sometimes it feels like my whole stomach is burning. I also get bad cramps when passing stools and bad upper stomach pain on the right too. The pain also reaches to my chest and I also suffer with heart burn.

I came away quite relieved that things were heading in the right direction and that my symptoms were real and not in my head. There are times you start to doubt yourself but I felt I was being listened to by both my consultant and GP. It was now a waiting game again with waiting for results and for my appointments to come through.

The following week I needed to see my GP as my preventative antibiotics needed to be switched and so I had some different ones to take for a further month to prevent my urine infections until my urology appointment came through. I filled her in with the hospital appointments from the week before as well as being concerned with new symptoms that have now just begun for me. I am now severely constipated and can't pass any stools. I have been in a lot of pain and all food and drink was hurting. I have been advised to go up to the maximum dose of Movicol to help me pass stools easier, but as of yet nothing has happened. She warned me that if the pain gets bad and I get high temperatures that I may need to be admitted to hospital. So I am now being even more careful with what I eat and drink and I'm hoping that things start to settle down. The pain is slowly easing but my stomach is severely bloated.

I get so down and confused with how my body can change so dramatically. I hope I will understand this disease more as time goes on, but every day is so unpredictable, I hate not being able to plan things in advance as I never know how I am going to be and whether things will get worse or not. There was one occasion when a friend of mine who helped me look after my daughter after school for one of my appointments at hospital asked me if I could look after daughter but she asked me the day I was due to see GP about my constipation, so I had to turn her down as I was unsure what would happen and whether my pain would ease or not. I feel so guilty saying no to my friends especially when they are always helping me. I am getting so bored with the unknown now and I am sure my friends and family must be feeling the same.

However, life goes on and I have to remember that there is always someone out there much worse than me. So I continue to put that fake smile on my face and carry on regardless.

Fifteen

Christmas arrived and luckily for me and my family, my symptoms did not get in the way of us enjoying our holidays. We managed to see lots of friends and family and also went to the cinema and theatre. We managed to have a relaxing time and it was also the first year John had nearly two weeks off over Christmas so we managed to get proper family time.

I noticed as soon as we got home and I was back to caring for the children once John returned to work that my symptoms returned, so it proves that stress is now becoming a major trigger of my stomach issues. This is something I will have to work on over the next year. I have already decided to exercise more to try and lose some weight, and to try everything I can possibly do to reduce my stomach symptoms.

It is now January 2015. The children returned to school happily and I received my surgeon and urology appointments which are within the next month. I am starting to feel quite scared, but also glad that they are drawing nearer so that I can finally get some answers about what is happening. Over the Christmas period I had another phantom urine infection. By that I mean I had some symptoms but nothing showed in the sample I gave to the doctor. I then looked back at the dates of the last few infections and when I last had symptoms and there is a pattern in when they appear, every nineteen to twenty-one days. I have booked to see my doctor so I can talk about this further as I am wondering if it's due to my menstrual cycle and whether gynaecology should become involved again. Due to having serious period problems I no longer have them and I take the pill constantly so I never know exactly when my cycle is.

By the time I saw my doctor I felt like I was having another urine infection, however I sent in a sample and nothing showed in the results. When I saw my GP, she recorded all the times that I have been to the surgery regarding my urine concerns and all the times samples have been done and the results they had shown. I was also by this point feeling very nauseous and getting bad diahorea. My GP felt it was due to being on antibiotics for a long time so she decided to stop my long term antibiotics and put a note on my records to only prescribe if urine comes back positive of infection. I was relieved of this as my medication list had come down slightly.

It was around the same time that my Methotrexate treatment changed from syringe to preloaded pen, which was slightly different to how I had been injecting myself before. I had been shown previously a long time ago how to use the new injections but I had forgotten so I saw one of the nurses in the GP surgery who showed me what to do. It was good to know I could rely on the nurses for reassurance as well as having a good trusting relationship with them all.

My stomach problems were slowly getting worse, despite being on two drugs for the reflux, nothing seemed to help. I was struggling at times to eat solid foods as it would sometimes hurt, or I would choke on foods. Sometimes even water was burning my throat and stomach. I decided to put myself on a liquid diet for most meals. This meant having warm milk with cereal as well as making or eating more soups. John and I also bought a blender to make my own soups as well as trying smoothies. I have found doing this has eased some of my symptoms but I realise that this cannot be done long term however until I hear about my gall bladder operation, I am prepared to do it. I tried juicing but this caused my acid reflux to get worse, so at least this way having the milk inside to line the stomach it's allowing also for me to manage and tolerate more fruit. I feel so much better for it and slowly my energy is getting better. Don't get me wrong though, I still have unpredictable days where the fatigue from the Crohn's hits me hard, but I now have come to accept this will always be the case and so I listen to my body on those days and rest. I have also started to do more exercise and have bought an aerobics DVD, so I can do it on my own at home with curtains closed not having to feel embarrassed. I do a fifty minute workout once a week as well as continuing to do my thirty minute walks every day. I have also stuck with cutting out the sugar and caffeine and using more natural sugars from fruit, honey and maple syrup. However as of yet it's not made much difference weight wise. But I have noticed some trousers getting looser. I hope the weight will all of a sudden drop off however as of yet this has not happened. I've noticed my lump in my stomach (Hernia) is more noticeable again, which is probably from where my waist may be getting smaller so my stomach is more noticeable.

It is now the third week in January and my surgeon appointment has finally arrived. It felt weird seeing him again as I never imagined seeing him so soon as it was nearly two years since he operated on me to do my reversal operation. On examination he could feel where the Gallstones were causing tenderness of my stomach, but he looked concerned. He realised I looked worried by his face, and he explained that he was just thinking about the operation as he said it was more noticeable that key hole surgery would not be able to be achieved due to the scars and incisions from previous operations. He said they may try it but he wanted to warn me that it was more likely it would be open surgery as he was also unsure whether my stomach and bowel would be stuck to the gallbladder. I felt worried but relieved as I wasn't really sure whether the surgery would happen because although my symptoms were getting worse, nothing was showing in my blood results however he said he was more comfortable doing this as there are no complications to the Gallbladder and it makes it slightly easier knowing that my liver and pancreas are not showing any signs of infection. I filled and signed the consent form there and then. I asked how soon the operation would be due to having a planned holiday abroad in May. I was reassured that it would happen well before May, which although reassured me being before my holiday, it slightly scared me too. It was also explained that due to it most likely being an open surgery, there was also a chance he would repair my incisional hernia at same time as removing the Gallbladder, which could mean two to three days in hospital and a two week recovery time. I was given lots of information on what to expect from surgery and after which was useful to have to show my family. During this appointment I was also asked to do some of the pre-operative assessment checks, so my height, weight and blood pressure was checked, and I was then told I should receive two letters in the post, my pre-op letter which can be completed over the phone, as well as my letter with the date of surgery.

It was a draining afternoon but as I have already said I came away relieved and worried; relieved that the surgery would happen and so most of my symptoms should disappear after this, and due to Crohn's being in remission I should hopefully be in a better place health wise to carry on enjoying my life and having more control of what I do with it. I also felt worried as I wasn't expecting the surgery to happen so soon.

However it not long dawned on me that this would be my fourth operation since diagnosis and as much as I now look at things in a more positive light, I can't seem to stop myself from thinking about the "what if's"; what if there are complications during surgery; what if I don't recover as quickly as planned like before? Luckily for me this time, those thoughts did not remain so deep seated and I was able to brush them to one side of my mind and continue looking at all the positives it could bring for me.

My friend M understood my concerns, I didn't even mention them to her, as soon as I updated her and told her I was tired the day after the appointment, she understood how draining those appointments can be and how we would focus on the "what if's" as any surgery is risky especially once you have had so many procedures. It was nice to have M there who understood without me having to say anything, I am not sure yet again what I would do without her, I think we are both each other's lucky charms, and she feels more like a sister to me these days than a friend.

Sixteen

I am going to take this moment to talk about normal family life, as quite a lot has happened. John and I seem to be getting along much better and we are communicating more often than we were. Our sex life is still non-existent but I am starting to feel more urges now, however John has eased off and is prepared to wait now until after my next operation and once we have some answers from urology. This has eased the pressure that I was feeling and relieved my stress.

Financially things are still a struggle as usual, but luckily the way I budget monthly is helping us save some money, however at times it's hard to not be spontaneous when shopping and it feels horrible having to say no to not spending extra money as I have to be disciplined.

John is working hard as usual and is planning on doing a fundraising event in the summer so he is now training hard on his bike and on his gym in the garage in preparation. He is doing the London to Brighton cycle ride with his old work mate from Essex. He plans on raising money for Crohn's and Colitis UK, which is good as it takes the pressure off me to fundraise this year and I can focus on getting fit and healthy instead.

I have a few resolutions this year and the main one is to focus on me more, including making more time to exercise and to hopefully socialise more (stomach depending as I still have unpredictable symptoms). Also this book has helped me with the next instalment by looking at life differently and helping me to be more positive. It is definitely helping me, as I feel calmer, however at times especially after my Methotrexate treatment I have my stressful times. It has also helped me remain more relaxed when organising all of our social events on the calendar. I no longer get stressed when new things arise or when things change. I am still impatient but that is different to feeing stressed. I like being in control of things which is why I have made a decision to choose what to do about my diet and go on more of a liquid diet for a while.

The children are busy too with school and all their out of school activities. Our son will be starting his swimming lessons again and has a few events coming up at school. Our daughter still attends her dance lessons, and is preparing for her exams. She has also been accepted to take part in a local pantomime, so she and 7 of her dance friends are performing in a local theatre. This means extra rehearsals and more routines to learn but she seems excited to do this. We applied before we realised my surgery was going to happen so quickly, but between me, John and my parents we have worked out a plan of how to get her to all the rehearsals. The dance school are also learning a routine to perform in Norwich for the Lord Mayors show. As well as soon preparing for their yearly dance show. They are also holding their yearly awards evening, so our daughter and I plus our friends from the school are planning to attend, as it gives us all a chance to get "glammed" up for the evening. It sounds busy; which it is, but very exciting at the same time. It really helps her release her inner feelings as I am sure she must at times get worried about what is happening at home, because there are times when my fatigue appears from nowhere so it must be hard for her and our son to understand.

They both have their birthdays coming up and I have managed to budget and organise their celebrations. Our son is having his first big party with his friends. And our daughter wants to go for a meal with us and four of her friends. I have been keeping busy preparing and organising it all. I just hope my surgery does not come in between it all.

I feel quite uneasy as I am still waiting for the date of surgery. I am constantly asked what is happening and I feel frustrated as I cannot give anyone an answer. My symptoms are getting worse, despite adding more liquid foods to the diet; however I am slowly reintroducing more solid foods so maybe that is why. I am back to square one where anything I eat is giving me stomach cramps afterwards and leaving me feeling quite nauseous. I am now scared of eating before going out in case I get sudden pains and urges to go to the toilet. So I am now having to eat a bigger meal at lunch and trying to eat smaller at night as I am now eating later which is against what hospital have advised me to do.

I don't feel comfortable going out as much now which I feel upset about; as before all of this and especially at the beginning of this book, my life was more on track and my social life in particular was returning, but I am sad to say that this is now not the case.   Crohn's and everything it comes with is so unpredictable and for a planned and organised person I find it doubly hard to manage.

I am relying on my hot water bottle and painkillers more often now and I am becoming very tired. The fatigue is hitting me hard throughout the day and evening, which is concerning me now. It was so bad one week that my exercise regime was non-existent.

I am trying so hard to stay fit and well but the combination of my drugs, my symptoms and everyday life is making it nearly impossible to allow me time to do the things I want to do.

I've booked an appointment to see my GP again about the fatigue which is another long wait. So I am back to the waiting stage once again; waiting for surgery date, waiting for my other hospital appointments and now waiting for the GP appointment. It seems to be never-ending, but as I now say; onwards and upwards. Only good things come to those who wait!

Seventeen

I read the last part of the last chapter back and decided I needed to be kicked into shape, this is not what my book intended to do this time round. So I decided rather than sitting and waiting I would carry on and fight through it as I have done for the past year. I managed to get back into my exercise video and surprised myself by managing a little more of it than usual.

I also had our daughter's birthday to concentrate on. She had a great day and we and four of her friends went out for a birthday meal. The evening was a success and although I suffered that night and the following day it was worth it seeing her so happy with her friends. She loved all of her presents that we and her friends and family bought for her. Luckily for me and our daughter, her birthday will continue into next week as both of us are going out for another meal on our own and then watching the ballet at our local theatre. It's nice to get to spend some quality time with her on her own, because as I have probably said, we don't get as much as we should together. I like having good things like this planned as it gives me and my family things to look forward to. We also have another girl's night out with her dance friends and mums because we are off to their dance school's awards night. I'm sure this has been mentioned before but I really treasure those moments.

These events took place, and are now over with. We had a lovely time with her dance friends, and also had a lovely day shopping and then seeing Swan Lake at the Ballet. We do not get much time together just the two of us. However I noticed my son has started to want to spend time with me. It is so hard getting the balance right and ensuring that I divide my time between the two. I made sure that I spent some quality time with him as well.

During this time I also received my pre – operative assessment letter for the 16th of March. It will be on this day that I will receive confirmation that my surgery will take place on the 26th of March. I also saw my GP about my fatigue and she said my blood results showed all was fine so as I was seeing the Rheumatology nurses very soon I should ask them about this. I added this to my long list of questions that I already had for them and I was surprised how quick my appointment was when I attended. My arthritis is in remission and they have no concerns and I can continue with my dose of Methotrexate. My questions got answered; she feels that the fatigue is due to the chronic illnesses working and fighting each other inside my body, but advised me to get my Ferritin (iron) levels checked at my next blood test. I am able to stop Methotrexate for one week during my surgery. As well as skip my treatment whilst on holiday. I am also switching the time I take my Methotrexate due to the tiredness I get soon after injecting myself; I am now going to be taking it in the evening rather than the morning.

I came away from this appointment feeling happy as I do not need to see the nurses until next year; I have never had a yearly hospital appointment before so it felt good knowing this would happen from now on, unless of course I get any problems in between which would mean me calling the advice line to speak to them and then maybe having my appointment brought forward.

As well as feeling happy I also felt frustrated because although one of my appointments have gone to yearly, I have an added appointment with Urology fast approaching. I have no idea what the outcome of this appointment will be, as it will depend if anything is found or if anything concerning requires further investigation.

This urology appointment was not attended, as before the appointment I ended up getting excruciating pains the night before and it resulted in me going accident and emergency with my mum. I have never experienced pain like this before in the whole 4 years I have had either symptoms or my illnesses. The best way to describe the pain was it was like labour contraction pains one hundred and ten times worse though. I could not get in any comfortable position and no painkillers were helping. My parents and husband were concerned so off I went. We felt it best to leave John at home with the children to make it more stable for them.

When we arrived I went to the desk and explained my symptoms, it was not long after that I was called into triage, as soon as I described my pain and went through my long list of past medical history I was sent straight away onto the accident and emergency ward. A nurse came over immediately and then I had to wait for a doctor. This part took longest but as soon as he saw me I couldn't believe how quickly things moved. I was rushed through to have canulas put in for IV fluids and painkillers and I was rushed through for an emergency chest and stomach x-ray. The doctor scared me as he seemed quite concerned with what was happening to me. Although it was not a pleasant feeling to experience, it was a relief to know that I was right in deciding to attend tonight. It's a hard decision to know whether to go or not. The doctor told me the x-rays showed a lot of gas and air in my bowel, so I needed to be admitted for further investigations. I was admitted onto a surgical assessment ward where I was seen by doctors. It was very late by this point and I was feeling more ill, in worse pain with extreme nausea and I was vomiting green bile constantly.

My mum was still with me and I didn't like seeing her so tired and worried, I felt awful I had made her feel this way but there was nothing I could do. I kept apologising to her as well as thanking her for being with me. She decided to wait until the doctors had seen me so that she knew what the plan was. It was not long until the doctors visited and as soon as he arrived I vomited again. Some would say perfect timing so they can see what was happening, but for me it was just pure embarrassment! Anyway they decided I needed to be in hospital and that this was a possible gallbladder infection and maybe also my bowel could be inflamed. I was put on IV antibiotics and they gave me an ECG (heart trace test) to ensure that there was nothing else underlying happening as well.

I stayed on this ward for a few hours in the night, but the doctors and my surgeon (with his lovely reassuring sense of humour told me that we should stop meeting like this before our surgeries!) decided that it was best to go on a surgical ward. I ended up back on the ward in the bed opposite where I was when I had my last operation.

I ended up staying here for a further five days as my symptoms were just not improving. I tried eating but I was just being violently sick all the time. I stayed on all IV medications throughout my stay which was draining and tiring. M visited me and we ended up calling my IV pole Percy, because it kept jigging around like an old man! Sorry if any elderly take offense to this, it's not intentional it's just my crazy sense of humour and a sense of humour is certainly something that helps get you through!

I had an ultrasound around the third day on this ward, but by then the symptoms were finally easing and the scan only showed that the Gallstones were infected so all the other inflammation had gone down thanks to the medications. The doctors explained to me that once I was eating again I would be able to go home and I would need to return as planned for my operation, they were unable to move this forward as this would be too risky for me, they don't like operating on patients with high inflammation and infection as it causes further problems which would mean longer recovery. I completely understood and felt reassured that they had my best interests at heart and that I did not need to rush home if I could not eat. It was a scary time being unable to eat and just being sick all the time, especially as the colour was not that nice either.

The only thing that bothered me was being away from my family and children, but I knew deep down they were in the best place and in safe hands of my parents and John. They visited me a few times and it was lovely to get cuddles with them as well as I am sure it was just as lovely for them.

By day five, I was much better and was keeping small meals down so I was allowed to go home, John brought me home and it was a weird feeling being home but a relief too.

I was lucky to have so much support whilst in hospital. Between my parents and husband they looked after the children and got them to school. My daughter had all her pantomime rehearsals which I should have been doing myself but my friend whose children were also in it managed to take my place and drive and chaperone everyone to their rehearsals. I felt awful not being able to do this but my friend was good enough to take my place. It is great knowing I have good friends like this around me and I have no idea how I could get through these unpredictable flares without them. I had another couple of friends who visited me in hospital which made me feel all warm inside, but sad also as I don't like my friends seeing me in that ill state. I have other friends who have offered to help with the school runs and dance lesson trips which I immensely appreciate as I still have no idea on the night that this attack happened how I managed to drive my children home okay as the pain started whilst at my daughters dance school waiting for her to finish her lesson and costume fittings for the pantomime that she is performing in.

When I returned home from hospital social media was filled with lots of get well messages; which overwhelmed me again.

Eighteen

I have been home for two days and I am feeling really tired and drained, I have severe headaches and I am feeling very clumsy. I am assuming it's the infection as well as all the medication I am now on for it that has caused this. My tummy feels tender and sore; I suppose I was not expecting to feel this way as I thought this would be the case after the operation not just after an infection. I am fortunate enough to again have my parents and John helping me.

I ended up plucking up the courage to book a doctor's appointment as I feel I need some Buscopan as my bowel spasms after I eat. However I was surprisingly given liquid morphine.

I also had to reluctantly cancel helping with the school's PTA (Parent, teacher Association) and doing the voluntary work with the school until further notice again. It makes me feel such a failure. Hopefully I can continue soon with this.

It has now been a week since being home and I've lost a total of one stone in weight since being admitted. I feel better for it but slightly concerned. I am now on a restricted diet until my operation which means it's very likely more weight will be lost. As much as I needed to lose the weight, I really did not want to do it this way. I am hoping the weight will stay off this time round after surgery. I have not struggled much with the diet I am now on so I hope I can continue as best as I can with the diet afterwards however adding the slight additions occasionally of chocolate and cheese as it's those I am struggling to avoid the most right now. Sucking on boiled sweets and eating bars of chocolate are just not the same. However meal-wise, replacing chips with boiled potatoes has been easy and I like boiled potatoes so I know most foods will remain with me and there are foods I will not miss knowing now how much fat they have in them. I have had to do this to reduce the infection in gallbladder and bowel returning before my op otherwise they will not be able to operate. I am being strict with my diet also as it was a scary time being violently sick and the pain was horrid, I never want to experience pain and sickness like that again.

I managed to see my daughter and her friends perform in their pantomime. It was a wonderful night, and very emotional watching them all dance so beautifully. The dance school posted photos regularly on social media which was reassuring to look at and to see how much fun she and her friends were having throughout the whole of the pantomime experience. However it is all over now but their next adventure is already beginning with the children starting to prepare for their yearly show. I am relieved in knowing that she will cope well with the longer days at the dance show as she has managed well with the pantomime days. She has made a lot of new friends doing this and I am happy for her to know that she has a new set of friends she can have fun with. I now need to concentrate on my son's hobbies. Luckily his swimming lessons start again; as he missed a whole term due to the boiler being broken at the pool. He also has his birthday approaching and he has his party soon; so I shall make sure that he gets a lot of attention during this time.

John has a long time at home which is nice and it has allowed me to do a lot more resting after coming out from hospital. He has been doing the majority of the school drop off and pickups but I will join him soon enough for these. I've worked out I will only have six to do on my own once John returns to work before my surgery, and then luckily when I get discharged about four days after surgery (I have been warned that due to my recent hospital admission , it is now possible my hospital stay for the surgery could be longer). It will be the Easter holidays. I also have my birthday before surgery however due to my restricted diet we decided it was best to celebrate mine after the operation once I am able to eat more foods again.

Our son's and my birthday has been and gone and we all managed to celebrate well considering what happened before hand in hospital and with my restricted diet. Our son had a lovely party with his friends and seemed to have a great time. My birthday felt strange but it was nice to do nothing and to just rest. I know that once surgery has happened I will get to celebrate my birthday again.

Six days after my birthday the day had arrived to have surgery, I did all my preparation such as washing in the hospital soap which I was told at my pre op appointment is to prevent MRSA. The children were staying with my parents and school were aware of what was happening as my parents had to take them to school. The morning of surgery I felt quite relaxed as I was relieved that it was finally happening. I thought the three weeks would drag from being home after being admitted, but they actually went very fast. Of course I had moments where I felt scared and I even had flashbacks of my previous surgeries as well as nightmares of what could happen within this one. It was my husband on this morning that was nervous, I could tell this as he was nonstop talking about anything and everything. I felt bad that I was making him feel this way and I hated knowing my family were all worried about me and the guilt sank in.

When we arrived I handed my letter in and I was told what ward I would go on and that I was second on the list this morning. I felt relieved that I would not have to wait too long. However things didn't go this way as I ended up being about third or fourth on the list and did not get called until half twelve in the afternoon. The waiting with having to starve from the night before was hard. However there were a few around me in the waiting room who were in the same position as me. By the time my name was called and I had to change into the gown and stockings I just felt happy I would now be able to get the operation over and done with. It was reassuring seeing my surgeon before hand as he has operated on me three times before. I felt safe knowing I was under his care in the theatre and knew he would look after me. It was time to go down, John walked with me as far as he could and then we said good bye. I was led by quite a good looking theatre assistant through to the anaesethic room, as I walked in I saw double doors opposite me and fear set in as I knew what was through there and I knew what was coming next. I had to lay on the bed to get all the wires and monitors attached to me. The assistant kept talking to me who made me feel more relaxed; we talked about our children which helped me lots. It felt like a life time in this room and then eventually the anaesthetist entered and it was time to put my canula in ready for the anaesthetic. I warned them that my veins were not great and they had to try twice as the first one in my left hand didn't work once it was in. Once the second cannula was put in and it was confirmed that all was ok, another man came in who told me it was time for me to sleep, the next thing I remember was waking up in recovery and I met a lovely nurse. It didn't take long to come round from the anaesethic however I needed to remain on oxygen as my SATS were still quite low. We ended up talking quite a bit and I found out that her daughter also had Crohn's. I felt at ease knowing the nurse in recovery knew about what I have got and that she would understand my pain and suffering. It did not feel too long after that I was wheeled onto the ward where John was waiting for me. He looked happy and relieved and I reassured him that I felt fine. The nurses handed over and she then helped me up so I could use the toilet and I was told that I could get in my own pyjamas. It was a nice feeling getting into my own clothes that had the familiar smell of home on them. I felt quite dizzy so I was sent back to bed. It was explained to me that I could go home tonight however they felt it was best to stay overnight due to me having young kids at home. I was told to only eat a light diet for a couple of days. John stayed with me for a little while until it was time for him to collect the children as he was off the following day so he could bring them home and take them to school. The evening went quite quickly, and I was not in too much pain, however the wind pain was the worst. I managed to do a lot of walking around which helped. My parents came to visit that evening and it was lovely seeing them happy when they saw how well I looked. We were all relieved that the surgeon managed keyhole surgery which I must say now having both keyhole is the better option. I was surprised that they managed due to my scar tissue and adhesions however I felt happy that I had a good surgeon who knew my body well so managed to do this for me.

After they had visited I walked around the ward some more but due to feeling dizzy and tired, I tried to get some sleep. However it was hard due to the lights and noise. I had to call the nurse a few times as well because I felt sick and was in a lot of pain, but after having some anti-sickness injections and some liquid Morphine things settled. The following morning, I managed some breakfast and I saw my surgeon who said I could be discharged and advised me to take off the dressings in five to seven days; I was able to shower as the dressings were waterproof and the stitches were all dissolvable so I didn't need to see the nurses for follow ups unless my belly button got very red as he warned me that out of the four incisions that the belly button would be the most likely to get infected. I thanked him for helping me and after two more hours, once the nurses visited and explained that my medication was ready I could leave. As John was not able to collect me straight away I was able to wait in their Day-room until he arrived.

I managed to get dressed in my clothes ok and I was surprised that my belly was not very swollen; as I was expecting it to be rather swollen as that has happened after my previous operations. I suppose that is another good thing about having keyhole surgery. John finally arrived and I collected my discharge letter and medication and we left to go home. The ride home in the car was quite uncomfortable, but better than I had initially expected.

Being home felt good and I felt in high spirits. One week on from my surgery I still feel the same way. Everything seems to be going well, and I no longer get many symptoms or pain. My constant nausea has disappeared and I am not getting much pain before needing a toilet. Between my parents, John and my mother in law, I managed to get a lot of help at home as well as my friends helping me by taking the children out for the day. I felt blessed knowing that my surgery went better than I first thought, my recovery was very quick and I had so much help on offer to me. However the only slight shock and disappointment I got was when I had to remove my dressings, and noticed that I no longer had a belly button as it was sewn up. It felt sad but I felt if that needed to be done for me to feel the way I do now then so it was worth it. I did go to see the nurse at the doctor's surgery to check my wounds as it was the Easter holiday weekend and I felt uneasy leaving my wounds unchecked for over four days. I was reassured all was fine apart from a small lump where my belly button was. I was advised to monitor this lump just in case the stitches do not dissolve there.

I am now another week on from this surgery and life feels great! I feel more positive and happy about the year ahead, so much so I am even thinking about job hunting soon or looking at some courses. We celebrated my mum's birthday and its John's very soon; we plan to go to the cinema. We also plan to take the children to the cinema during the second week of their Easter holidays as well as a family meal out. Then we plan on visiting friends and need to celebrate my birthday. I am sticking to my low fat diet as it's really helped me lose my extra weight that I had managed to put on as well as it helping with my stomach.

We only have 7 weeks until our holiday to Spain and it's given me something to work towards. I really want to enjoy this holiday properly and I hope my energy remains as high as it is right now so that I can do some fun things with the family whilst we are away.

Nineteen

The Easter holidays have been and gone and we managed to have some great family days. I even managed to take the children out on my own a few times which is a big achievement for me. The children ended up having some good memories to share and I am pleased that things are finally going well for us. Our daughter had an audition to star as Elsa for a TV company and was called back to a second audition. We are all very proud as she made it into the top twenty overall. Considering twenty-five thousand applied and eighty took part in the first audition. She really enjoyed doing it and has now found something else she would like to do as well as dancing, which is acting. Our son is starting to get more involved in the physical activities when at the park, which is an achievement for him due to his asthma. We celebrated John's birthday over Easter and we had a lovely day together. Overall as I said before our holidays were great this year and it will not be long before we go abroad again, back to the place we went four years ago. The holiday resort we stayed in that I shared about in book one.

However as we all know alongside the happiness always comes some kind of worry when you have chronic illnesses. I had a urology appointment, which although went well I am still at square one as to what is causing my urine infections. I had to have a Cystoscopy (camera in the bladder) to check if there was inflammation or any fistulas. Luckily enough the cystoscopy showed nothing, so I was advised to self medicate on antibiotics whenever I got symptoms. I also have to send in urine samples each time too to check for infection. In three months time if I still get symptoms but samples come back clear I need to see them again.

The Cystoscopy itself was a bit uncomfortable but I am now used to these procedures so I feel I am able to cope a lot better these days, however although I was warned about them, the after effects were bad as my bladder felt very sore and I was in severe pain when passing urine. It lasted about two days. The urologist did say that sometimes the Cystoscopy itself can stop further infections from happening so I am hoping this will happen for me, but only time will tell.

I also have another appointment to attend very soon, something I have not shared yet in my story, one because I am trying to keep my book as positive as I can, and two I have no idea what the problem is if there is one, and whether it is really related to my Crohn's. However as we all know by now if you have read my previous book especially, that with Crohn's you just don't know what it can do to our bodies, so here it is, another problem to add to my list, but I'm hoping that it's something very mild and not too serious.

I have been experiencing a lot of tenderness and swelling around my left armpit, and I've noticed that my left breast is a lot more swollen and a different shape to my right one. I have seen my GP a few times now about this and she felt also when examining them that the left one was more tender. She ended up referring me to the breast clinic at the hospital. The letter has arrived which then shook me slightly as I am seeing a breast surgeon who is based where my other surgeon is. I'm assuming that they are all under the same clinic. Anyway

I am probably over-reacting but the unknown still scares me. Yes I know I should be well used to all of this now however I still experience rare moments of anxiety.

This anxiety though has caused my sexual fears again and I am still unable to share intimacy with my husband. John and I ended up arguing over this however since explaining my fears and anxieties he understands, but it doesn't help me with feeling so guilty about this area of our relationship. I know he understands and knows it's not because I don't love him as I certainly do. I just don't have much confidence in my body, and with this added problem I still don't feel ready. It gets me down as I wonder whether I will ever be ready and whether my body will give me a complete break from it all.

That little gremlin keeps making its appearance when you least expect it too, the anger of having this awful disease makes an entry and doesn't just shock those who you end up shouting at but it shocks you too. You hate the person you have become for this short amount of time that the anger reaches boiling point. Then you feel angry for allowing the gremlin in and making you feel that way. As well as the frustration that the illness (even though you are in remission) is still getting in the way of the things that you want most of all.

The anger lasts minutes but the after effects can last for days. You then become quiet and withdrawn and embarrassed, you end up spending the next few nights unable to sleep, you feel bad for making him feel awful inside and you wish that you could rewind the time back so that you could start that moment all over again.

My dearest friend M was there to help me through this sad part and I feel so thankful to her for helping me. She goes though enough as it is without having to listen endlessly to my problems too. I am always there for her too, but it does feel that she does more for me lately than I can offer to her. However this will change now that I am recovering well and enjoying life again.

Luckily this was a little blip in my life and things are still going positively well. I have my date for my breast scan as I saw a consultant who reassured me it was nothing to be concerned about and the scan is a precaution. I need to take evening primrose oil as the symptoms are most likely hormonal.

I have ended up with another urine infection however my sample came back clear, I have been advised to see the urologist again in three months to see if they can do further tests.

My stomach still occasionally flares but I am no longer in constant pain.

I have noticed a big difference especially when going to visit friends. Even though I am still watching what I eat, as I've said the pain is more bearable and I get little twinges rather than sharp stabbing pains. I am now beginning to enjoy life again. So much so that I've enquired about two jobs, I hope that one of these will be suited for me.

Everything seems to be going in the right direction for us all at last. We still have some minor appointments to battle through soon but finally they are becoming less and less and I am finally feeling more positive about the times ahead whether they are good or bad. I'm no longer worrying about the bad times as I know I can fight it now. I have been though a lot worse things and I know of others who have been through worse. I now believe I can overcome anything!

Time is going on and I am still feeling great. I have a few outstanding appointments and scans but I am continuing to feel positive about this and I am ready to face the next lot of challenges.

I have no idea what those challenges will be but one thing I do know is that I am ready for them and this time the gremlin will not get in the way!

I think this is a good way to end this story. It is hard to end my story now as things are very good, but I feel I have shared all that I can with you. Thank you all for spending the time reading my story and I hope that not only it has given you an insight of living with chronic illnesses but you have somehow enjoyed it too.

So good bye for now!

Overcoming ongoing struggles

I spoke quite a lot about my triggers and ways to overcome these hurdles in my first book. And I felt it was best to carry this section on into this book too. As you have probably noticed from reading my next chapter of being in remission, I have still had hurdles and obstacles to cross. I know life in general is not simple and I am no way saying that we have it any harder than anyone else, but I hope people get an idea of what we go through as all symptoms of IBD are not visible and obvious to the human eye.

Stress and Diet

My main two triggers are still stress and diet, but as you may have noticed my mental illness are in a much better place now. It happened so quickly and writing my first book helped immensely with battling my depression and anxiety. The gremlin inside is still there but is very small now, I have no idea if my headaches now are to do with the gremlin shrinking, is it the gremlin banging for attention, who knows? But all I do know is I am trying hard to not give it any.

However although mentally things seem brighter now, I still find stress makes me feel worse and there are times I don't feel mentally stressed but I start to flare in my stomach and joints. Stress is a very horrible thing and can cause so many problems, I have tried to overcome them as much as I can but this is an ongoing battle as well as my chronic illnesses.

Anxiety is still causing a lot of my symptoms too, and it's a strange feeling to describe when I get anxious, worried, scared or upset; my stomach all of sudden feels like it's exploding and I get excruciating stomach pains. I find I end up with diarrhoea and my urine problems arise.

As I've said diet still plays a huge part as I now have a diagnosis of IBS so foods can cause diarrhoea or constipation as well as nausea and bloating. It explains a lot of my issues with food and although there are foods that I know triggers my Crohn's (tomatoes, popcorn, nuts, raisins, sweet corn, grapes, strawberries, lactose, mushrooms and red meat, wholegrains and seeds, skins from fruit and vegetables). There are foods I know can cause me IBS problems too which vary on a day to day, such as caffeine, sugars, sweeteners, gluten, onion, garlic, processed foods, and frozen potato products.

I now tend to make my own foods especially burgers and meatballs and stick to egg noodles or rice or sweet potatoes rather than potatoes and pasta, I do eat them but they are classed as my treats!

I plan my meals for the family weekly which help me lots especially being on a budget and I find my children are becoming more adventurous in foods too and trying new things; which helps as we can all eat the same meals more often. I try as much as I can to just use my lacto free products in our cooking to make it easier. Mine and John's families also do the same so it is reassuring to know that most of the foods I eat are safe for me. Food shopping is slowly becoming easier and less expensive now that I know what I am looking for and now I am slowly realising what foods to stay clear of. I am still not 100% there and my symptoms are not really improving but somehow in my mind I am not as anxious about what I am doing so I hope that it is more the anxiety rather than the food that is actually causing the symptoms but I suppose only time will tell on that one.

Treatments and drugs

We will be constantly surrounded with treatments and drugs and even in remission I am still trying new drugs to relieve symptoms. My main problem still with most drugs is the horrible nausea and loss of appetite. It feels like I am constantly feeling sick, I wake up feeling sick and slowly by the time I go to bed the feeling has gone. I find eating little and often help with the nausea. I am still injecting my Methotrexate treatment, but I am now on more drugs since being in remission than I was at the end of writing my first book due to increased symptoms of headaches and having anaemia on and off as well as having recurrent urine infections and other ailments.

The main issues I now have with treatments are the extreme reactions I can get. I spoke briefly about this in book one that many drugs are given to overcome side effects. However since having severe reactions I am becoming more reluctant in trying new drugs. In my first book I was developing a food phobia and now it has switched to a drug phobia. It now scares me when they suggesting trying new drugs. However I now trust my consultant when he suggests trying a new drug for my stomach issues, fingers crossed this goes ok!

I still have the same problems with pain relief and can still only take Paracetamol. It's not good to take this long term as they can cause their own set of issues.

As I have already said, I still inject weekly and have had no problems with doing this. My nausea from this medication has finally gone, but I do know if I was to be increased on it then the nausea would start again, most other drugs can cause nausea too. I have also begun getting very moody and snappy after taking this drug and I seem to get a lot more colds. It is making me wonder whether this is the right drug for me so I am in the process of discussing these concerns with rheumatology.

I am no longer having any pelvic problems and the birth control pill I am on has resolved all of my gynaecological problems that I talked about in my first book. The only effect from this that it is causing some weight gain. However I am reluctant to come off this as it is helping with my periods and has also stopped triggering flare-ups at those times too. However I have now developed new pelvic problems which are more bladder related; only time will tell on what happens there.

When taking these drugs and looking at what all the drugs do to me and my body I wish there was just one drug that covered it all and was 100% safe with no reactions at all. I do realise that I am actually dreaming and that I don't think this would or could ever happen.

Exercise

Exercise is still a constant battle, however the practice walks and the sponsored charity walk have inspired me to start up a weekly walk, I aim to do three miles one day a week and may try some of the cross trainer that is sitting in my garage. As I said in the first book, I really struggle with exercising due to my constant fatigue. I don't have a lot of energy and feel like I need to save my energy for when the children are home and to do the housework, cooking and school walks every day.

I have started gardening again and I suppose this could be classed as exercise too. I find gardening therapeutic but I also found the walking around the village doing my practice walks a good therapy too. Who knows there may be a Marathon walker in me yet!

Like my diet, I find if I do a little exercise at a time, this seems to work better for me, so I try and do a little exercise a day. I am trying to find the energy to do my exercise videos which will enable me to do my exercises in the comfort of my own home without feeling embarrassed and also I will not have the added stress of comparing myself to others in the classes. The exercise routines have been going well and have gone better than expected. I have also allowed myself to stop them when I feel my body needs a rest and now after surgery I am still finding the right time to start them up. Again, time will tell when my exercise regime begins again.

Work

Now at the beginning of this book going back to work was a big goal for me to achieve however this is my biggest dilemma due to my current symptoms. I have started doing more voluntarily work at the children's schools but sometimes with my low immune system and feeling generally unwell or exhausted I do not always manage it. As well as also having hospital or doctor's appointments which are sometimes on the same days! These sometimes puts me off the idea of work and whether employers would take someone like me on, someone who needs constant time off for appointments. There are days I have lots of energy and other days I struggle with small activities that it makes me wonder whether I could manage a regular job anymore. I struggle as it is taking care of my two children full time let alone adding a job to that equation.

Then there is the discussion of money, I wouldn't want to be put in the situation as what we were in before when I was working and calling in sick but not getting sick pay. If I worked my ESA (Employment Support Allowance) would stop so I would have no income to contribute to the house. We struggled extremely badly last time that I could not risk doing that again as we were fortunate enough to have some savings behind us, but this time round we do not have that luxury.

I hope that I manage to return to work as the stigma of being on ESA which is not income based just national insurance based is horrid. I am certain people think I am abusing the system but I am not, I am only getting what I have put in all those years ago when I was working as the ESA is based on how much national insurance I have put in since working. I try to avoid talking about this to people as I hate explaining my situation over and over again.

I feel grateful I have been able to receive this as I know some people do not get any help but it hurts when I get tarnished with the same brush as others who are on benefits. I hope by writing these books people will understand that there are different types of benefits for different circumstances. Everyone always wants to be treated fairly but I know this will never be the case for us all. I would not say I have been dealt a fair pack of cards over the past few years.

I think the reason I struggle with the ESA stigma is that I have always been a hardworking person and have worked since leaving college, even working in the evenings too. I found it hard and still struggle now with not being able to work how I used to and even considering going back I have to think things through so thoroughly with regards to how I would manage the routine of a job with this unpredictable and demanding illness. Normally I would be happy to accept any job offered to me, but with this chronic illness it is not always that straight forward and with other extra ailments and illnesses on top. The recent eye scare made me realise how messed up my body is and that I can react badly to drugs. This all would make it near impossible to fulfil and hold-down a full-time job whilst trying out new drugs as I couldn't guarantee how my body would react.

I still am aiming to return to work as soon as I know how I will recover from my my most recent surgery. The thing with my illnesses is that I never know what will happen, and nothing ever goes to plan. As much as I am, my friends, and family are all remaining positive all will go well, somewhere at the back of my mind I am mentally preparing myself in case something happens and things don't turn out the way we are all expecting them to.

However this goal looks like it may be within reach sooner than I first thought. I have applied for a local job plus enquiring about working in a local school. I can also say that I have begun my voluntary work in the Infants school again so this will give me some experience again.

New meal ideas

As I have said, I now make most of my own burgers and tend to use pork mince or turkey mince and use the leanest meat possible. I bind my mince with egg yolk to keep the burgers or meatballs together and I keep them in the fridge for thirty minutes to help them cook better and so they don't fall apart.

I fry them but I use the spray olive oil as it is better for me.

I bake lactose free cakes and biscuits fortnightly, which allows me to have some sweet treats occasionally. It also allows me and the children to spend time together and we get a lovely reward at the end too!

Apart from these there is not much I am doing differently as my IBS and stomach pains are milder now than what they were in my first book, so I have felt that whatever I was doing in my first book has finally worked. Using the low fodmap diet is also finally helping me, and although cutting out onion, garlic, cauliflower, some wheat, as well as the fructose, glucose and sucrose was difficult, I am now finally seeing the benefits. I also have cut out more sugar and replaced with more natural sugars such as honey and maple syrup. I don't feel as bloated and my stomach cramps are not constant anymore, I still get them but I go through periods where they appear more often; all of my symptoms have been appearing more higher up in my stomach now with my acid problems.

I no longer have juice as I felt that this was aggravating my stomach. I think the acid and sugars inside were causing this. However as stated above I now make soups and smoothies, using my new blender to make them. Here are some good recipes I use on a regular basis:

Berry and Honey

200ml of lactose free milk (alternatives can be used)

Handful of raspberries

Handful of blueberries

A small spoonful of honey (unsweetened)

Protein Smoothie (my husband's favourite!)

2 bananas

Handful of strawberries

2 tablespoons of peanut butter

300ml milk

These are the two bases for any smoothies; you can add whatever you fancy or whatever you fancy. I have added mango to my berry smoothie.

There are lots of vegetable smoothies to try to such as

Go Green

1 avocado

Handful of chopped spinach

Cucumber

Ginger and turmeric

Apple and pear slices (peeled and cored first)

200ml of milk

Again you can remove and add whatever you wish to, trying different milks is a good way to add taste also, and I have been advised to try almond milk.

You need to check out my soups in my first book. I now blend these in my blender to make them finer which I am finding suits me better.   I am occasionally managing to tolerate onions and tomatoes when finely blended which is a good base for any soup.

Ideas on how to help children cope with their emotions and feelings

I spoke briefly about this in my first book, and felt that I needed to add it to this book as I have been asked by a few people about how the children have coped throughout my surgeries and illness and scares. I was fortunate enough to have worked in a Children's Centre and I did lots of one to one work with children on dealing with their feelings and emotions so I was able to use what I had learnt from my previous work with my own children. It was not a nice feeling realising that my children were suffering inside and I felt guilty as their mother by not being able to prevent this from happening to them. However I have finally realised that this is just part of growing up and part of their development.

The main thing that worked for my daughter was the Worry Tree, it could either be a 3D tree or one that you have drawn where you can either hang or stick on your worries. It also does not have to be a tree it can be a bear or dolly or flower, or anything that your child is interested in. I also ensured my daughter had a "happy tree" too as I did not like focusing too much on the negatives but looking at what makes her happy too. I allowed her to choose a private place for this, and she showed me where it was going to go. It was reassuring to know that she wanted me to know where it was and it was a good way for her to communicate to me her worries without actually saying them to me. It really helped during the times I was in and out of hospital. Once we knew her worries, we were then able to sit with her and reassure her about her fears and explain to her what would happen during these times. We now do not use the trees we just sit and talk things through. However there are times I can tell she does not want to talk so I occasionally remind her of her trees.

You can also adapt these trees to any emotions such as an Angry Tree, Scared Tree, Sad Tree, Happy Tree.

If you are more creative and have good joints to do more intricate things, worry dolls or teddies are good too, and getting the children to help make them, you could knit and sew these dolls with them.

It has taken me a while to realise why my son does not require or rely on the worry trees like my daughter does and that is because since birth he has a muslin blanket which he either snuggles with or puts in his mouth. I have a feeling that this blanket is his worry or anxious blanket and uses that at times when he is tired, anxious and or worried. I need to try my best to remember this for when he starts or tries new activities. However he has not required it for school so that's a good sign he is settling ok. He does have his blanket a lot at home, and at times it makes me feel guilty that home life may make him anxious; I need to refocus and accept that this is normal, and it's a natural feeling to have. I just hope we all learn ways together to overcome our anxieties in a safe way.

There are lots of activities you could do too such as play dough, drawing painting and sand and water. These are lovely relaxing ways to express their feelings. The size of paper is essential for their different feelings. If you want to help control their anger give them small pieces of paper so that they have to contain their drawings in a small place and will help them concentrate more and should relax them. Sometimes large pieces of paper are good if they become hyperactive as they can then create in a large space and get all their ideas and hyperactivity out of their system.

I also like doing goal sheets with children as this can help them work towards goals they want to achieve, it can be anything from what they want to do when they're grown up or a trip they want to do or something they want to save their money for. I also like planning with my children so I get them to draw a spider-gram of things they want to do and things we should take on our picnic or on trips out. It is a good way for us as parents to organise outings but getting the children involved too.

I also find crying in front of them helps too. It may seem an unpleasant thing for children to see, but actually from my experience it helps them learn that crying is ok and should not be hidden. Crying should not be seen as a weakness but as strength. I don't just cry and then leave it, as that would cause my children to worry, instead once I have calmed down I explain why I was crying and why I was upset, this has helped my daughter and we now are slowly getting a closer bond as sometimes our hormones and emotions occur at the same time and we end up arguing. It is hard when you are in the moment and we do have those arguments, but I always ensure that we have time after to talk it through. I listen to her too and we try and understand one another better together.

I ended up buying both my children a Worry Bear and a Worry Owl for them because they are not using their worry trees at all anymore. My daughter loves her Worry Owl and it's helped her not worry or get upset as much, it has also helped her calm down a little bit so now she is not as anxious. My son also loves his Worry Bear and cuddles it all the time, I'm not sure that he fully understands what it is for like my daughter but he seems very pleased and proud of his bear and makes sure he has it in his bed every night before going to sleep.

It is reassuring to know that my idea has seemed to help; I just hope this continues for a long while, as I feel that will need them in the near future.

Outline for a Happy Tree

(Write or draw happy thoughts amongst the leaves or around the edge)

Outline for a worry tree

(Once again write or draw worries or unhappy times within the leaves or around the tree).

Alternatively they may want to draw their own as some may have different ideas of what happy and sad trees really look like to them)

"I wish"

Here is a short poem that I want to share in this book with you all. It was another moment of instantaneous inspiration, very similar to the one I got when I wrote my first book. It pretty much sums up my feelings over the past four and a bit years since I have felt ill.

When reading this it sounds quite depressing, but I'm sure a lot of people wish the same things, it's only because you know a lot about me and my illnesses that it might make you sad when reading this. Please don't feel sad when reading it, that is not my intention, I just found it a good method to sum up some of the feelings I can experience. I don't feel this way always, but I only seem to come up with these poems and books on my "down days".

As much as it is hard to read, it is very hard for me to write these negative feelings down on paper for everyone to see.

I realise that happiness is whatever we make it and I intend to fill my life with more happiness so I hope you find the end of this book uplifting!

I wish

I wish that I could feel normal

Even for just one day

I have so much I would like to do

And so much I have to say

I miss doing all the good things

That I should be doing in life

I want to be a better mother

And a more loving wife

Where have all my good times gone

They disappeared so fast

I wish for these times again

So they are not just a part of my past

I wish there was more to life

Than taking drugs day and night

I'm determined to not let it beat me

And to stay strong and win this fight

I wish more happier days would hurry

I have so much I want to do

I would love to be that person

I was when I first met you

By Nicola Martin

Letter to my children

To my loving children;

I am sorry I haven't been able to do all the fun things you are missing out on. I am also sorry for my constant mood swings.

I am sorry for making you worry about things that no young child should have to think about.

I want you to know though that despite those times I love you so much and you will always come first in my life and I will be here for you regardless.

I do thank you both for all your patience with me and for helping me lots. I love all the kisses and cuddles we share together, and I treasure those precious moments we have especially when you tell me that you love me and I am a lovely mum.

I hope like me you remember all the good times we share together. Everything we do is to give you many happy times that you can remember forever.

I want you to know I will never give up and neither should you. Never think that you cannot achieve something, always try and believe in yourself and hope that anything is possible in life.

Things will change now as I am slowly getting better and I hope to become a stronger and happier mum. Someone you have not really met yet. You have only known me as someone who visits hospitals a lot with needles in my arms and hands. Those pictures of me will hopefully fade as time goes on, but remember those times as your mum who kept fighting. Something I hope will pass on to you both. Keep fighting for your dreams and goals!

I am looking forward to spending more time with you and sharing many more happy times together.

Thank you for giving me something to fight for and together now we can carry on fighting.

Good bye to the sad and worrying times and hello world! The world is ours, we can be finally free. Let's embrace it while we can!

But you better hurry up children and try to keep up with me!

I love you both so much xx

Lots of love Mum xx

Epilogue

Well it is that time again where I have come to the end of my second book, I have no idea whether there will be a third as I am going to give this part of my life a break and concentrate on some other ideas I have for children's fiction books as well as some interesting fundraising ideas I have.

I have thoroughly enjoyed writing my life down for everyone to see, it has been a great form of counselling for me and it has been stress-free as I have written it in my own time whenever I have spare moments. It was fascinating how this book ended up being written as more of a diary entry but hopefully this has been an interesting read. As I've said I really hope this book and my first book can help raise more awareness of not just Crohn's but other invisible and chronic illnesses. I have not done this to gain sympathy but to give everyone an understanding of how life can actually be when living with it. Before diagnosis I had family who lived with it but never fully understood what it was like until I become the one living with two illnesses myself.

I also hope that you have noticed how much more positive this book is to my first and I hope it gives people hope that life can be better and illness is not all full of doom and gloom, even with all my health scares I am still here and looking at things brighter and sunnier! It has been hard but I hope whatever struggles you go through in life, that you can fight those nasty gremlins away if you put your mind to it. Anything in life is possible, it's just a case of knowing and realising when you are ready to face them and battle through them with confidence.

I never thought that the day would come when I could say I have no gremlins, because really, I do not have them now; of course I have my down days, but I have had to take some big risks in life, some were easier than others, but overall they have helped me to overcome the mental difficulties of what these chronic illnesses can leave us with.

Also I want to give some advice in general and some words of wisdom to take away with you. They are:

- Follow your dreams - I have and look at what I have managed to achieve, I never thought my dream would come true in publishing books.
- Never give up - even when life looks very dull and you feel life is not worth living for, keep going and keep fighting as there is always something worth fighting for, even if it seems small to others, it can be the biggest for us!
- Life is not a competition – never compare yourself to others, I've learnt the hard way, it will only push you further back and you are only giving the gremlins more power. There are a few people who treat life and their illnesses and struggles as a competition with others but how is that going to give you the confidence to fight them, it is only going to make you realise how worse or better off you or others are and will make you feel sad and more helpless. I now have realised everyone has their struggles, not everyone has the same but to that person they are just as important as what ours are. It doesn't really matter what they are, it's just being able to offer everyone the same friendship and support and reassurance that we are here for people. Whenever I talk about my woes I don't expect people to help and solve my issues, but just some encouragement and reassurance is all it takes for people to move on in their life.
- Achieve one goal – find a goal big or small and carry it through, which is the one thing I learnt from my wellbeing counselling sessions, and it's the one thing that has helped me get to where I am now. Once you have achieved one goal it will give you the encouragement and confidence to do more
- Never judge anyone - as much as we all do it, it is a horrible feeling being on the other side of it. No one really knows what someone is going through inside, lend a hand, a cuddle or your ear and wait for that person to come to you. I know I am not the most patient person in the world and this is something I am still learning to do more in life
- Learn to accept life - This is a tough lesson to learn, and I still struggle with this. However with having two illnesses that at present have no

cure, I have had to accept that this is the way my life is, I can't change anything about it, so I may as well just live with it. Of course I can have some control of my illnesses by choosing what drugs I put inside me and choose how much or little I do activity wise. I still need to overcome this lesson by ignoring others around me who upset me. Some days I can do this easier than other days but if we can ignore others and accept that we are who we are, then hopefully others will accept us too, and of course realising that there are just some very selfish people out there who will always look at their life as worse than yours. I am proud to say I am not that sort of person and accepting ourselves and the way others are will help us move further forward in the right direction.

- The last and most important is to have fun! - I try and have as much fun as my illnesses will let me, I suffer afterwards but it is definitely worth it to see not just a smile on my face but smiles on my family around me. It can be something as big or as small as you like to have fun, it could be just starting a hobby up that you had forgotten about. Such as reading, writing, drawing or something else. Life is too short to just stop everything in life.

So I will now say goodbye for now and I may see you all again, who knows what the future will bring, all I can do is hope for a cure for not just Crohn's and IBD but for all those other nasty illnesses and diseases out there who cause too much suffering on those who have it and their families who have to deal with the aftermath every day.

Additions

From completing my book to getting it ready to publish, a year has passed and the reason for this long delay is due to a few significant life events, some good but as always with me some bad.

So I thought I would take the chance to fill you in from April 2015 to the present day of sending it to the publishers. I could have saved it for book 3 but as I have said I am not sure yet if I want to continue and also some of the past year has been a "blur". Here is a brief account of what has happened.

April 2015 –recovering from Gallbladder operation, urology appointments, had ultrasound at breast clinic; all was fine for both and discharged from both. Over time my urine infections stopped.

May 2015 – Family holiday which was one of the best I have had since diagnosis of Crohn's because I had more energy.

June 2015 – Received confirmation that I had got the job at our local High School. Also started Adult ballet lessons where my daughter goes.

July to September 2015 – Had a lovely summer holidays visiting people and going places.

September 2015 – Started work at High School.

December 2015 – Had an almost symptom free Christmas, had a lovely time spent with family.

January 2016 – Started experiencing breathing problems, had a couple of trips to the doctors

February 2016 – Nearly collapsed at ballet due to having trouble to breathe. Went doctors following morning referred to Respiratory department and sent for urgent tests and x-rays, all ok but some concern over my peak flow tests.

March 2016 – tests done at Respiratory department. Our daughter had her yearly panto show where she was a dancer again. I was suffering from chest infections, started on inhalers for what they felt was Asthma

April 2016 –Stomach and reflux problems started again, had a ph level test (tube down the nose into stomach) which was very unpleasant. Diagnosed with

GORD (Gastro Oesophageal Reflux Disease). I was already on maximum dose of medications so I needed to continue as I was. Colonoscopy booked too to check Crohn's had not become active.

June 2016 – Colonoscopy was done, it showed no active Crohn's but was a very difficult procedure for the surgeon and I was in a lot of pain for this one, it was discussed that it could be adhesions and scarring that was causing it.

July 2015 to September 2016 – Had lots of fun and made lots of memories, went on a lot of family outings such as Harry Potter World, Lego land, Windsor Castle, trip to London to Madame Tussauds and National History Museum, seaside trips and visits to friends and family.

Also in this time I saw my Gastro Consultant who decided that it was time for me to have an operation for my reflux as it is getting progressively worse. On examination the consultant found an Incisional Hernia in my stomach. So I am currently waiting for an MRI scan to see what size it is and whether there are any adhesions near it so that they can operate on this also.

As well as this M became very ill and I was visiting her as much as I could in hospital and then finally in the Hospice. During this time she also sadly passed away and she has recently had her memorial service. I have been struggling to come to terms with it all at the moment which is why it has taken a while to get this book ready however the time has finally arrived.

I am definitely going to say good bye now but it is not forever I am sure. As I have said before being in remission does not mean we are cured or are better, it just means that the "nasty" Crohn's has decided to stay quiet for a while however all the other issues that it and the past operations have caused have decided to cause more problems. Life is certainly a challenge and we really must make the most of it as we never know what the future will bring! Take care everyone and it has been a pleasure sharing this with you all!

Thank you

Firstly I want to thank my special friend M for just being there all the time for me; I want to say that I will always be there for you too. It feels like we have a special bond and a unique friendship that words cannot properly describe. I've said this many times before but you are a true inspiration to me and you are the reason that I maintain a positive outlook of life. You are also like a blessing and my guardian angel in disguise and I will always remember those twinkles in your eyes in December 2012 when I saw you for the first time when I came back from my life saving operation. I care so much about you and wish you all the best for the future.

As I said at the beginning I dedicated this book to M as by the time I got it ready to be published she sadly passed away. Thank you to M's family for allowing me to continue with this book and also thank you for all your support over the time I have known M, I know our relationships with each other will continue for a very long time.

Thank you to my longest friends Karen, Rhiannon and Autumn, we have known each other for over thirty years and have always remained friends through the good and bad, let's hope for a further thirty years of friendship and many more too. Also thanks to Nicola for always being there for me, we may not see each other much but you are always there with inspirational words of wisdom, the friendship is mutual.

Next I want to thank two good friends Martin and Sophie; you have both given me the support and encouragement to go ahead with sharing my experiences. Your friendship means a lot to me. Thank you also Sophie for proof reading this book for me, your help on this book was much appreciated!

Thanks also to Kim, Karen and Naomi, you do so much for me such as listen to my moans and groans, help with looking after our children when we have appointments or when you notice I need a break. I appreciate all you do and I try my hardest to return the favours however as I said in my first book, I appreciate the friendship and that you always help without expecting anything in return.

I also would like to mention Karen, Melissa, Angela, Sarah, Helen, Nicola, Jackie, Claire, Lisa, Emma and Helen . You always offer me so much encouragement and have always got positive words of wisdom to give to me. You are all great friends to have so I want to say thanks for being there in ways you may feel you do nothing, which is what I appreciate most. Thank you also to everyone else who has been there for me for the past four years. I appreciate everyone's support.

There are three people who I would like to thank and they are Sheri, Brandy and Stephanie, I feel blessed to have found you on my support groups on Facebook and I have also managed to meet Stephanie in the flesh at the Crohn's and Colitis London walk. Thank you for all your support on the groups and for offering good advice when needed.

I would also like to thank my "Fab Facebook Friends"; Mandy, Sarah, Jessica, Claire, Joanna, Samantha, Tracy and Angela. I may not have met you all, but I feel blessed to also know you from the support groups on Facebook. Thanks also for all your support and advice, and for the mutual friendships we share. It is reassuring to know I have people with similar problems around who understand exactly how I feel at times.

I must thank all my doctors, nurses', consultants and my surgeon again for all their continued good work, I may have been through a lot but they do a good job as best as they can to keep us all as healthy and well as possible. They have been very patient with me and listen well now to all my concerns and symptoms.

Again I would like to thank John's family for all their love, support and understanding and encouragement. I appreciate the way you have all accepted me into your family and it's a relief to know I have you all around at difficult times.

I would like to thank my parents next; words again cannot describe how much I appreciate all you do for me. You are both my best friends as well as my parents, and I owe you so much as you have made me into the person I am today. Without your support, love and encouragement I am unsure whether I would be the person I am. Thank you also for all you do for us and our children. We all appreciate the time you spend on us.

Thank you mum for being not just my mum, but for being my best friend and a sister to me. I love you so much and wouldn't want to change anything that we have as you are a wonderful role model of how mothers should be to their children. I hope I can be the same with mine.

Thank you John for everything you do, you are such a great husband and dad and friend as well at times, a carer. What I love most is you never mind doing the extra things that no person should have to do. Here is to many more years together and I appreciate how hard you work to provide for us all. I also want to say that I love you so much; I don't say it enough and I find it hard showing emotion publicly, so here is me doing this publicly now, "I LOVE YOU!"

Finally I want to thank my two beautiful children who mean the world to me. I feel blessed having them in my life and I thank you for being so patient with me. I treasure the moments you both say I love you and you are the best, and I want to say that you both will always come first regardless of how well or ill I am at times. You are my world and I will always do what I can to keep you safe and happy.